SERVICE LEARNING ACROSS THE CURRICULUM

Case Applications in Higher Education

Edited by

Steven J. Madden

University Press of America,® Inc.
Lanham • New York • Oxford

Copyright 2000 by
University Press of America,® Inc.
4720 Boston Way
Lanham, Maryland 20706

12 Hid's Copse Rd.
Cumnor Hill, Oxford OX2 9JJ

Library of Congress Cataloging-in-Publication Data

ISBN 0-7618-1583-X (cloth: alk. ppr.)
ISBN 0-7618-1584-8 (pbk: alk. ppr.)

Contents

iv

Preface

Steven J. Madden

Never before in the history of education have people been so aware of the connection between pedagogy and our communities. Non-profits, for-profits, local, state, and national government entities, the CEO of a multinational company and the farmer just outside the city limits continually inform us how service learning projects have impacted their lives. The professor's life as well as the student's has also been impacted. We must all understand basic citizenship processes if we are to know how our world became what it is, how it is organized, why it changes the way it does, and ultimately our role in this creative endeavor. Such knowledge is valuable not only for those who make great decisions, but also for you, since this is the world in which you live and make your way.

This book on service learning has been designed to 1) offer project examples that teachers and students in higher education can explore, 2) show the complexity of service learning with its interconnection between community service and learning goals, and 3) illustrate how teachers and students seek personal growth, social growth, intellectual growth, citizenship, and preparation for the world of work through various methods of serving the public.

As you study this material, you'll find yourself looking at educational and human behavior in a different way, for teachers and students involved in service learning don't simply volunteer. Instead, they blend service and learning in such a way that both occur and are enriched by each other (Toole & Toole, 1992). Since students don't live in an educational vacuum, they must act in relation to others outside the classroom. Thus, teachers and students interact with the needs of the community through an exploration of the relationships between theory and application - service and learning.

Chapter One

An Orientation to Service Learning

Marty Duckenfield & Steven J. Madden

   Readers of this book will explore a fascinating array of approaches, learning systems, and project methodologies that can be used in creating service learning components for their own classes. The discussions are presented in an applied format based on actual service learning projects bridging multiple disciplines across a university campus. One unique feature of this book is that almost all of the service learning projects can be adapted to work in a multitude of other curricula. Hence the material covered here has broad utility while carefully maintaining a focus on academics. From the beginning of this century visionaries realized that in order for our society to grow and prosper we needed a strong base in education, service, and citizenship.

   Service learning has been an emerging teaching methodology with deep roots in a variety of important movements spanning several decades. In 1915 William James called for a corps of young people to serve the country in a fight against social injustice. In the 1960s and 1970s the Southern Regional Education Board and the federally supported University for Action (UYA) also became active in launching college level service learning programs. Throughout the 1980s we saw the formation of a student service learning organization known as the

Campus Opportunity Outreach League (COOL) and an organization known as Campus Compact created by college and university presidents. Finally, in 1990 the National and Community Service Act was established. As advocates of each of these movements find their philosophies converge, the support for service learning has grown exponentially. Service learning is a method that not only stands on the shoulders of John Dewey's thinking in experiential education, it also incorporates such important educational concerns as personal and social development, citizenship preparation, and career education.

Experiential Education

The roots of service learning are certainly found in the Progressive Educational Movement led by John Dewey. Formal education had evolved over time to become the traditional model of passing a pre-determined knowledge base, whatever the discipline, on to a new generation of students. The methodology of this transmission is familiar to all of us: lectures, chalk and blackboards, reading, and written examinations. The professor is the source of information, and the student absorbs what he can. Inspired by Dewey, a new generation of educators initiated a variety of interpretations of his theories of education, especially including experience as the teacher. Many extreme versions of interpretation led to the total abandonment of traditional education, with totally free experiences becoming the vehicle of learning.

In response to these interpretations, and with a reiteration of his own educational philosophy, John Dewey, in *Experience and Education* (1938), shows how education is not an either-or- proposition. One does not need to choose between the two extremes, and in fact should not. The knowledge base is indeed important. But certainly experience in interpreting that knowledge, testing it in current situations, and analyzing its meaning is crucial for true learning to take place. Indeed, a student's natural interest in a subject can only be sparked by an involvement in the subject, and therefore immediate interaction with the new knowledge in meaningful ways is needed for successful learning. It is the task of the educator to provide those experiences for his students that will be a "moving force" for real learning and understanding to take place.

Personal and Social Development

Dewey's philosophy on experiential education provides a strong foundation for other important experiences contributing to the development of young people. The personal and social development of youth through the experiences of community service and reflection on those experiences is the focus of Robert Coles' *The Call of Service* (1993). Building on his own experiences as a Harvard undergraduate— Coles was involved in providing mentoring and tutoring service to children from ghetto areas in Boston in the 1950s—and his later involvement in desegregation efforts in the South in the 1960s, he shares stories of personal growth in moral development of the students of the 1990s as they too discover the lessons to be learned about themselves, their role in society, and the issues that impact what society has become. This personal and social growth has come about from firsthand experience and reflection guided by a more experienced elder such as a teacher. College-age youth are at an age where interpretations and understanding of important moral issues can be greatly enhanced by direct involvement in solving problems in the community.

Citizenship Preparation

Benjamin Barber, in *An Aristocracy of Everyone* (1992) envisions that in our American democracy, the college will take seriously its role in the development of good citizens. In order to become good citizens, he maintains, students have to *practice* being citizens. Under his leadership at Rutgers University, a curriculum was designed to integrate experiential learning in community service or other team projects for the purpose of developing citizenship abilities through solving community problems. Barber considers that mere volunteerism is not an antidote to the preponderance of civic apathy; it alone cannot teach the skills needed to become a good citizen. An education-based course, however, targeting the development of civic responsibility, helps students understand the needs of the community at large. They also gain an understanding of why it is in their self-interest for their communities to be healthy and their role in accomplishing this. Through an academic course, citizenship skills can be taught while what is learned through simple volunteerism is altruism or charity, an important distinction. Advocates of civic education, like Benjamin Barber, believe that as educators of the future leaders of a democracy, higher education institutions have an obligation to include an academic course in civic education.

Career Education

At many institutions, especially community colleges and universities preparing students for careers, long-term work experiences such as internships have provided students with opportunities to apply their newly acquired skills. Similar to the European model of apprenticeship, American students actually leave campus for a semester to participate in the workplace to hone their skills in a real-life setting. In many instances, such experiences tend to lengthen the duration of the undergraduate experience as classes and internships take place in isolation from each other. Nevertheless, universities have supported such experiences as positive, and students not only gain opportunities to apply their knowledge; they also make connections that provide them with very useful references that future employers find most valuable!

Blending These Together

When we blend community service with reflection, civic education, and career education together on a foundation of experiential education, surely we create what Ernest Boyer has called the "New American College" (1994). His vision shows a campus where faculty collaborate with community partners, where the classroom is indeed without walls, and where students participate in field activities which connect ideas they learn in their classes with real life. We have what is today called "service learning."

For service learning to thrive in higher education, it must first be understood that service learning is a successful teaching method. Then, if this is felt to be true, the fact that service learning does even more only adds to its appeal. For what is extraordinary about service learning is its capacity to weave in these youth development needs with the required academic curriculum, enhancing that curriculum and deepening its impact on the student.

The Service Learning Framework

What has emerged today as service learning can be captured in a simple framework: Preparation, Action, Reflection, and Celebration (Duckenfield & Wright, 1995). Each of these four components adds important dimensions to this unique form of experiential education. Carefully followed, the framework assists the novice and advanced practitioner alike as they strive to produce that educational experience for their students that will have a lasting and meaningful impact.

Preparation consists of learning experiences that take place prior to the actual service. Students are involved in identifying and analyzing a problem, selecting and planning a project, and receiving appropriate training and orientation.

Action is the service itself and needs to have academic integrity, be meaningful to the student, provide for student ownership, have adequate supervision, and be appropriately challenging.

Reflection enables students to think critically and analytically about their service experience. A structured opportunity needs to be provided where students can reflect through discussion, reading, writing, production of products, or the arts.

Celebration is the component where students are recognized for their contributions. It is also an important time for closure, particularly needed when direct service with other people is going to be ending.

Next Steps

Opportunities abound for faculty to test service learning within their own subject matter. As Edward Zlotkowski states in his challenging article, "Does Service Learning Have a Future?" (1995), the onus is now on those faculty who have tried this evolving teaching pedagogy to share their experiences with faculty at their own institution, through journal articles in their own disciplines, and to the higher education community at large. For it is through this sharing of knowledge that the next steps in improving education for our postsecondary students can take place.

The stories in this volume reflect the teaching experiences of faculty at a land-grant university, Clemson University. With funds from the provost's office supporting innovative teaching methods, a faculty-student Service Learning Collaborative was formed to raise awareness of service learning at Clemson while at the same time providing training and mini-grants to support attempts to integrate service into existing curricula. This faculty, who received either monetary or moral support (or both) from the Service Learning Collaborative, share their successes, dilemmas, and solutions with the reader, thus providing the field with some fresh ideas and new approaches to help promote this application of learning.

Case Applications

Chapter Two: Psychology by Patricia Connor-Greene. This case application describes a problem-based service learning (PBSL) project designed to enhance student learning in an Abnormal Psychology class and provide a service to the community through the creation of mental health resource guides.

Chapter Three: Horticulture; Planning and Landscape Architecture; and Sociology by M.T. Haque, L. Tai, and B.J. Vander Mey. This is a case study involving the creation of sustainable landscapes for a low-income community. Students enhanced their education in landscape design and implementation through several partnerships, which resulted in the creation of a certified backyard habitat for low-income residents.

Chapter Four: Public Health and Parks, Recreation & Tourism Management by Jennifer Hinton, Francis McGuire, Judith Witthoeft, Jessyna McDonald, and Deb Mitchell. This service learning project involved health promotion for the aged and focused on three primary goals: (1) Assist traditional university students and older persons in learning concepts of health; (2) Provide these two groups with the opportunity to interact in a service program and establish a reality-based perception of each other; and (3) Provide a service to the communities participating as service learning sites.

Chapter Five: Nonprofit Marketing by Patricia A. Knowles. This case application discusses service learning projects that concentrated on conducting a marketing analysis for a nonprofit organization. Additional emphasis covers clients, students, project assignments, and learning benefits.

Chapter Six: Organizational Communication by Steven J. Madden. In this project students from two separate classes conducted an organizational communication evaluation of four organizations including a police department, a public works department, a fire department, and a youth agency.

Chapter Seven: Business Writing by Elizabeth C. Rice. In this service learning class students gather "issues" from their community and work toward solutions in interdisciplinary teams. Ultimately, the students create a "deliverable" for their client and present their project in a multimedia trade show to their peers, faculty, college administration, and their client.

Chapter Eight: Science by J.R. Wagner and E.R. Caldwell. Elementary, Early Childhood Education, and Special Education majors participated in a series of service learning formats and venues focused on the sharing of science experiences and projects with elementary students from numerous sites.

Chapter Nine: Education by Carol G. Weatherford and Emma M. Owens. This case application discusses how pre-service teachers are provided opportunities to experience service learning as a valuable teaching tool emphasizing how classroom learning to real classrooms and real students is an important goal of teacher education programs.

Chapter Ten: Technical Writing by Barbara Weaver. In this technical writing class, students engaged in service learning activities resulting in the creation of brochures, Web sites, published articles, and public service announcements for a variety of clients.

Each of these case studies explicate the variety of service learning approaches that can be utilized in the college classroom. The underlying assumption in this book is that each of us has the ability to grow personally, professionally, academically, and with a sense of civic responsibility. But an even greater goal is for us to accomplish these objectives together. If this book makes even the smallest positive difference in your life, your class, and your community then we have done our job. Believe us when we say that these service learning projects have tremendously enlightened our personal lives and the lives of countless others.

Works Cited

Barber. B.R. (1992). *An Aristocracy of Everyone.* New York: Ballantine Books.

Boyer, E. (1994, March 9). "Creating the New American College." *The Chronicle of Higher Education.*

Coles, R. (1993). *The Call of Service.* New York: Houghton, Mifflin Company.

Dewey, J. (1939). *Experience and Education.* New York: The Macmillan Company.

Duckenfield, M., and Wright, J. (editors). (1995). *Pocket Guide to Service Learning.* Clemson, SC: National Dropout Prevention Center.

Zlotkowski, E. (1995, Fall). "Does Service-Learning Have a Future?" *Michigan Journal of Community Service Learning.* pp. 123-133.

Chapter Two

Psychology

Patricia A. Connor-Greene

Abstract

This chapter describes a problem-based service learning (PBSL) project designed to enhance student learning in an Abnormal Psychology class and provide a service to the community through the creation of mental health resource guides. Students gain in-depth information about a specific psychological disorder and its treatment, investigate bibliographic, internet, and community resources, and determine the availability and appropriateness of local treatment options. Student groups select resources and treatments they would choose as if they were actually dealing with this disorder within their own family. The project shifts the emphasis from the teacher as expert to the students as active consumers and evaluators of information and resources.

Service Learning/Problem-Based Learning Framework

One of the rewards of teaching is seeing our students take information out of the classroom and into their lives, connecting academic learning to real-world experiences. The content we teach in a class today may be obsolete in a matter of weeks, months, or years; it is the *process*, the problem-solving, analysis, and synthesis skills that will endure over time.

In recent years, faculty across disciplines have developed teaching strategies to encourage active, hands-on engagement with course material. As John Hildebidle (1991) wrote, "the word learning is, properly, a verb masquerading as a noun: an activity, not a substance; something we do, not something we have."

Problem-based learning is a teaching strategy that had its roots in medical education at McMaster University in the 1960s (Neufeld & Barrows, 1974). The basic tenets of problem-based learning emphasize student-directed learning in small groups that work collaboratively, with problems serving as the starting point and stimulus for learning (Wilkerson & Gijselaers, 1996). For reviews of problem-based learning, see Albanese & Mitchell (1993), Berkson (1993), and Vernon & Blake (1993).

Like problem-based learning, service learning emphasizes active engagement in real-world challenges, linking together academic coursework and community issues. Service learning places academic learning in a broader context, requiring active application of principles and integration of theory and practice (Batchelder & Root, 1994; Duffy and Bringle, 1998; Eyler, Root, & Giles, 1998). In contrast to traditional classroom lectures, service learning facilitates moving from a stance of "knowing what" (factual knowledge) to "knowing how" (procedural knowledge), which is critical to the development of expertise (Eyler, Root, & Giles, 1998). Service learning fosters practical, usable cognitive skills, giving students the opportunity to test out their classroom learning in the real world. When doing fieldwork, one is confronted with multifaceted problems, questions, and controversies (Grose, 1990). Students who have participated in service learning projects show greater complexity in their grasp of social problems than do students who have been in traditional classes (Eyler, Root, & Giles, 1998). By helping students develop a more complex understanding of problems that they face as citizens and giving them experience in working collaboratively, they are developing "citizenship expertise" (Eyler, Root, & Giles, 1998; Kendall; 1990).

To encourage students to develop a real-world understanding of the complexity of psychiatric disorders and treatment, I designed a project for my Abnormal Psychology class that combines problem-based and service learning (PBSL). In this project, the problem-based element involves student teams seeking resources to deal with a specific psychological disorder. The service learning component is the team's creation of a resource manual to be used as a guide to resources and services for those in the community seeking mental health treatment. The project was developed to enhance student interest and learning, develop teamwork skills, increase empathy for those experiencing psychiatric problems, use student writing and team editing as a vehicle for learning, enable students to gain in-depth information about a specific psychiatric disorder and treatment, and encourage active group learning through investigating bibliographic and internet resources, visiting and evaluating community treatment facilities, and sharing this information with classmates and the community through the production of a resource manual.

Students often take a class in Abnormal Psychology because they are seeking information about psychiatric problems experienced by a family member, friend, or themselves. Although the Abnormal Psychology class covers a large body of information on psychopathology and treatment, its lecture/discussion format gives students little opportunity to develop the problem-solving skills needed to understand and find help for someone with a psychological disorder. To become educated consumers of psychological services, students must gain hands-on experience in locating and evaluating relevant information and treatment.

Service Learning is often conceptualized as containing four elements: preparation, action, reflection, and recognition.

Step 1: Preparation

The class (approximately 30 students) is divided into groups of 4-5 students, and each group randomly draws a card that specifies a situation (e.g., "your 18 year old brother has just been diagnosed paranoid schizophrenic"). Because the project is designed to mirror a real-life situation, assignments are random rather than chosen, because in reality, no one can choose whether their brother would be depressed or schizophrenic. Every situation assumes a family connection to the individual who has a psychiatric disorder, and a wide range of disorders are included. Each group then works together on a project that spans the semester. In the preparation phase of the project, the group compiles an overview of the disorder, along with a list of likely questions and concerns that one would have if indeed a family member faced this situation. This list should reflect an informed understanding of the challenges of the disorder, demonstrating that the students have begun reading about the problem.

Step 2: Action

In this phase, each group compiles an annotated bibliography of journal articles, books, and internet resources that address this disorder and its treatment. The annotated bibliography includes a reflective component, in which students write a brief justification for the inclusion of each citation. Because much of the available information may not be pertinent to the group's problem, the key aspect of the bibliography is *appropriate selection.*   Each group also investigates community treatment resources, including public and private facilities, self-help groups, and any other relevant treatment options. Students make site visits to those treatment resources in this geographic location that have been identified by the group as most relevant, and write site visit reports that address relevant issues (e.g., cost of treatment; provisions for those with no insurance or financial resources; description of physical setting including location, types of buildings, students' responses to this setting, both positive and negative; approach to treatment; medications (if any) typically used to treat this problem, side effects).

Step 3: Reflection

Throughout each step of the project, students write individual components and edit one another's contributions to their group project, providing written feedback and suggestions for changes. These changes and suggestions are then incorporated into a group component for each part of the project.   Each project also includes a summary and recommendations section, which summarizes the main treatments for this disorder along with their risks and benefits, an analysis of the adequacy of bibliographic and internet resources in helping family members obtain useful information, and an assessment of the adequacy of treatment options available in this area for helping someone with this specific problem. This portion of the project also addresses recommendations: what additional bibliographic materials would be helpful to individuals or families facing this problem; what additional treatment resources are needed; what book or article needs to be written?

Step 4: Recognition

In the final part of the project, each group revises and compiles all parts of their project into a bound volume. Each group member receives a copy, and any interested individuals in the community retain two copies for use. Each group presents its findings and recommendations to the class in the form of both an oral presentation and a written executive summary. The written executive summary is also posted to a computer class workspace shared by all class members. The entire class benefits from the in-depth information compiled by each group and learns about a variety of disorders and their treatment.

The Project / Assignment/ Objectives

The Problem-Based Service Learning (PBSL) project consists of five components spanning the semester; each part is composed of written individual parts that the team members edit and synthesize into a group product. Each team decides how to divide the work into individual parts. The five assignments are:

Overview

An overview of the disorder, including theories of causality, major approaches to treatment, and primary benefits and risks of each treatment, as well as a compilation of *informed* questions and concerns (i.e., reflecting an understanding of the disorder) they would have if their family member actually faced this situation, as well as a brief written overview of the disorder derived from library research (etiological theories, common treatments and their risks and benefits). Time frame: 1 week for individual contributions, 2 days for edits, 2 days for group compilation.

Bibliographic Resources

A carefully selected annotated bibliography of relevant journal articles, books, and internet resources that address this disorder and its treatment, including a brief justification for the each reference selected. Time frame: 1 week for individual contribution, 1 week for edits, 2 days for group compilation.

Site Visit Reports

An evaluation of community treatment resources, including public and private facilities, self-help groups, and any other relevant treatment options for this disorder. Each team visits facilities in the community that offer treatment for their project's disorder, and prepares site visit reports that address relevant issues (e.g., cost of treatment; description of physical setting including location, types of buildings, students' responses to this setting; approach to treatment; any relevant medications and side effects). Time frame: 4 weeks for individual contribution (with in-class discussion time at the end of 2 weeks for each group to discuss the adequacy of their sites so far), 2 days for edits, 2 days for group compilation.

Summary and Recommendations

An analysis of the extent to which questions raised by the team in Part 1 have been answered, along with new questions raised by the information found; assessment of the adequacy of information obtained in Parts 2 & 3; assessment of the strengths and weaknesses of existing bibliographic, internet, and community resources. Time frame: 1 week for individual contribution, 2 days for edits, 2 days for group compilation.

Bound Resource Manual

In the final part of the project, each team revises and compiles all parts of their project into a bound resource manual available to the community to use as a guide for better understanding this disorder and finding helpful bibliographic references and appropriate treatment. They also prepare a brief (1-2 page) executive summary and distribute this to other class members, so that every student benefits from the information compiled by each of the groups. Time frame: 1 week for group compilation (each part has already been edited previously; the revised parts comprise the final bound copy).

Reports

The first time I used the PBSL project, I gave verbal instructions for each of the five parts of the project, but did not initially provide written guidelines. As I read the first group of completed assignments, it became apparent that I needed to give much more detail to the students about my expectations and provide greater structure for the assignments. I developed detailed checklists for each part of the assignment, which the students turn in along with each part of the project. The checklists include information about both the structure (e.g., how to list references) and the content (e.g., specific issues to assess when making site visits) for each section of the project. The checklists accomplish three purposes: (1) clearly outline the requirements for each part of the project to the students, reducing their uncertainty about teacher expectations, (2) improve the final product by providing focus and encouraging appropriate detail, and (3) streamline the process of grading, as the checklists are then used by the teacher to indicate specific strengths and weaknesses of the project.

I have now used this PBSL project for four consecutive semesters, and have modified the logistics of the assignment each semester. The first semester, all parts of the project were completed as a group effort within each team, with no individual accountability. Predictably, there was considerable variability in the effort put forward by each group member. "Free-riders" and "transaction costs" are problems that frequently plague team projects (Yamane, 1996). "Free-riders" are students who don't do their fair share of work but reap the benefits of the team grade; "transaction costs" refer to the time and effort team members must spend arranging meetings, collecting and integrating information, and compiling a final product acceptable to the group. Both free-riders and transaction costs were obvious concerns during the first semester in which I assigned the PBSL project.

I modified the PBSL project to include both individual and group grades, which eliminates "free-riders." Each of the first four components of the project (overview/questions, bibliography, site visits, summary & recommendations) now include individual contributions from each group member, edits by each group member of every other members' contributions, and group reports reflecting these edits and changes. Each group report is then graded by the professor, and returned with written feedback. This feedback on each section of the manual is then incorporated into the final bound copy (part 5 of the project).

The issue of "transaction costs" has been alleviated by a new computer system at our university, the Collaborative Learning Environment (CLE), which provides on-line shared class workspace. Each member of the team can post individual parts to the CLE team workspace, which each member of the team then edits on-line; these edited parts are then compiled into a group product. The role of project manager (the one who compiles each edited individual part into the group product) is rotated among the group for each part of the project. The ability to communicate and edit documents on-line greatly reduced "transaction costs." Furthermore, with the advent of the CLE, the only paper used in the project is the final bound copy.

In addition to the final bound copy of the resource manual, students also give an informal oral report to the class at the end of the semester, and provide a 1-2 page Executive Summary (posted to the CLE) for their classmates which gives a brief overview of the disorder and its treatments, most beneficial journal articles, books, and internet sites, and their recommendations for treatment sites in this area.

Planned & Unplanned Outcomes

The PBSL projects resulted in student-created resource manuals for the community which deal with a wide range of psychological disorders including autism, obsessive compulsive disorder, agoraphobia, schizophrenia, panic disorder, attention deficit disorder, bulimia nervosa, social phobia, anorexia nervosa, generalized anxiety disorder, alcohol dependence, Tourette's syndrome, pathological gambling, marijuana dependence, bipolar disorder, and depression.

Comments from students both informally and on course evaluations indicate that the PBSL project has been a valuable addition to the Abnormal Psychology course. One of the most apparent outcomes of the PBSL project was the type and complexity of the questions students raised in class. Prior to PBSL projects, I had never been asked in class about mental health care for the indigent, problems with medication interactions, or questions about credentialing of mental health professionals; these became typical questions after implementing the PBSL projects. Asking questions is one indicator of active, engaged learning (Keeley, Ali, & Gebing, 1998). Student concerns and questions voiced in class (e.g., dismay at the lack of treatment sites in this geographical area for a particular problem, frustration at the "red tape" encountered when they try to get their questions answered at a treatment facility, shock at the high cost of mental health treatment, questions about how much insurance and cost drive treatment options) suggest that students have become acutely aware of the complexity of dealing with mental health problems.

After participating in the PBSL projects, students express concern about the lack of appropriate treatment for specific disorders and display more understanding and appreciation of risks of treatment. For example, a team assigned the problem of a 6-year old brother with Tourette's syndrome raised a concern about the risk of tardive dyskinesia (an irreversible neurological condition) as a side effect from a medication sometimes prescribed to treat this disorder. This team's response indicated a much greater connection to the course material than I had seen in classes prior to the PBSL project. The PBSL project helped to shift the student attitudes and behavior from detached academic interest to invested, concerned involvement.

In addition to changes in student questions and concerns, the degree of energy in the class suggests that the students are more engaged with the material and with one another as a result of the projects. Editing and commenting on team members' work on-line allows students to learn from and build upon each others' ideas.

Evaluations

Students completed anonymous evaluations of the PBSL project. Their written comments reflected the following themes:

Benefits:

- "working in groups - learned more, got to know others"
- "learned a lot about the disorder and how to find help"
- "site visits are especially helpful"
- "textbook can't give the detail that site visits do"

- "better able to see patient and family's perspective now"
- "lack of good treatment options is eye-opening"
- "it's encouraging that good help is available even if someone has no money"
- "we have a finished product that will help others and will help us in interviewing for jobs or graduate school"
- "going to sites that treat this problem made it more real"
- "more practical research than a term paper; useful information"
- "good preparation for graduate school"

Problems:

- "working in groups - hard to coordinate; not everyone contributes the same"
- "hard to find time to schedule meetings"
- "frustrating to try to set up appointments at treatment sites"
- "hard to find treatment resources"
- "some sites never returned phone calls"
- "time; there was often a long wait before talking with someone at a site"
- "have to drive to get to treatment facilities"
- "hard to know where to begin to find treatment"
- "had to call lots of places before finding one that offered treatment for this problem"

It is noteworthy that several of the problems cited by students are the same real problems faced by individuals and family members seeking help for an actual psychological disorder (unreturned phone calls, transportation problems, difficulty finding appropriate sites, not knowing how to find treatment, long waits). In this way, some of the frustrations experienced by the students were actually a central component of the learning experience.

Many of the student comments reflected a more complex and contextualized view of the psychological disorders and treatment; several examples are listed below:

The textbook does a nice job describing each disorder, but it does not do justice to every aspect. This project allows me to learn in detail and in context.

The site visits were the most helpful part of the project, but the most difficult.

I learned how to make contacts with the community when someone or me has a problem. I also learned how frustrating trying to do this can be.

This is the first time I have been to a treatment center, and I've been a psych major for 4 years! I think that any project that gets students out into the field would be a great help. I have not come across any material except the textbook before!

Benefits & Challenges of Service Learning

In assessing the educational worth of any project, it is important to consider both benefits and challenges. The PBSL project gave a "real world" focus to the Abnormal Psychology class, which provided a view of both the breadth of resources and the obstacles to finding appropriate treatment for mental health problems. In addition to the student comments already described, the level of class discussion in the classes that used PBSL reflected a broader, more contextualized view of psychological disorders.

This PBSL project included the challenges inherent in group projects. These concerns were alleviated by introducing a grading structure that rewarded both individual and group work. Communication within groups was facilitated by the use of shared computer team space. In settings that do not have access to this type of on-line team space system, it would be important to set aside class time for teams to meet, given the logistical problems of scheduling out of class group meetings.

Having students edit each others' work is important for several reasons: (1) they become familiar with all aspects of the project, giving them the "big picture," (2) they have an increased sense of ownership over the final product, (3) they see each others' edits and comments, and can learn from and build on each others' ideas.

The projects take time, both on the part of the students and the professor. Detailed checklists provide clear expectations, help students to focus their efforts, and streamline the process of grading. The checklists also provide guidance in what to look for in assessing treatment sites, which is important for those students who are unsure about what questions to ask.

Several treatment sites refused to meet with students and suggested that the students do library research instead, as their services and time were reserved for paying clients. However, most treatment sites welcomed the students and provided them with valuable information, especially when they realized that the students were compiling a resource manual to be used by people in the community.

Summary & Conclusions

This PBSL project is now in its fourth consecutive semester of use, and has been modified each semester to encourage both individual accountability and better team communication. The Service Learning Collaborative (SLC) at Clemson University played a central role in the modifications and refinement of this project. In the initial semester, each of the five PBSL parts were completed as a team, which allowed uneven distribution of effort among team members that often plagues group projects. In the second semester, a mini-grant from the SLC funded photocopy costs, so that each team member wrote an individual contribution to share with all team members; these were then edited by each team member and compiled into a group product.

This approach was much more successful in fostering meaningful work by all group members and encouraging team members to work collaboratively. However, two major challenges remained: 1) an enormous amount of paper was required for each student to edit multiple drafts of their teammates contributions (photocopy cost and paper waste), and 2) communication within the groups was difficult given students' busy schedules outside of class (meetings were difficult to arrange). The Service Learning Collaborative's Faculty Forum Series provided the key to solving both of these problems. One forum described the Collaborative Learning Environment (CLE), a computer-based system new to Clemson University that enabled classes to be grouped into teams which can communicate via computer and edit text on line. The information from this forum led to a grant from Clemson University's Advanced Technology Center Instructional Development Grant in the summer of 1998 to incorporate the CLE system into the PBSL project. The PBSL project currently uses the CLE system, which eliminates the problems of paper waste, printing cost, and scheduling group meetings. All team members now post their work on a shared computer workspace.

As a result of the PBSL project, resource manuals dealing with a wide variety of psychological disorders are now available to the surrounding community. To increase the accessibility of information and impact of the service aspect of the project, the next step in the evolution of this project is to create web sites, with appropriate links to mental health agencies, for each of the disorders.

In assessing the value of any class project, one of our best sources of information is feedback from our students. One of the students in the Abnormal Psychology class summarized service learning in this way: "I know my efforts are going to be used to benefit the community. I feel like I'm doing something to help other people - that makes me want to do a good job. The project has a point!"

Works Cited

Albanese, M. A., & Mitchell, S. (1993). Problem-based learning: A review of literature on its outcomes and implementation issues. *Academic Medicine, 68,* 52-81.

Batchelder, T. H., & Root, S. (1994). Effects of an undergraduate program to integrate academic learning and service: Cognitive, prosocial cognitive, and identity outcomes. *Journal of Adolescence, 17,* 341-355.

Berkson, L. (1993). Problem-based learning: Have the expectations been met? *Academic Medicine, 68* (10), October Supplement, S79-S88.

Duffy, D. K, & Bringle, R. G. (1998). Collaborating with the community: Psychology   and service-learning. In R. G. Bringle and D. K. Duffy (Eds.), *With Service in Mind: Concepts and Models for Service-Learning in Psychology*   (pp. 1-17).   Washington, DC: American Association for Higher Education.

Eyler, J., Root, S., & Giles, D. E. Jr. (1998). Service- Learning and the development of expert citizens: Service-learning and cognitive science. In R. G. Bringle and D. K. Duffy (Eds.), *With Service in Mind: Concepts and Models for Service-Learning in Psychology* (pp. 85-100). Washington, DC: American Association for Higher Education.

Grose, S. K. (1990). A student's advice on connecting community service to the college curriculum. In J.C. Kendall (Ed.), *Combining service and learning: A resource book for community and public service, Volume I* (pp. 483-492). Raleigh, NC: National Society for Internships and Experiential Education.

Hildebidle, J. (1991). Having it by heart: Some reflections on knowing too much. In C. R. Christensen, D. A. Garvin, & A. Sweet (Eds.), *Education for Judgment* (pp. 265-274). Boston, MA: Harvard Business School Press.

Keeley, S. M., Ali, R., & Gebing, T. (1998). Beyond the sponge model: Encouraging students' questioning skills in Abnormal Psychology. *Teaching of Psychology, 24*(4), 270-274.

Kendall, J. C. (1990). *Combining service and learning: A resource book for community and public service, Volume II.* Raleigh, NC: National Society for Internships and Experiential Education.

Neufeld, V. R., & Barrows, H. S. (1974). The "McMaster Philosophy": An approach to medical education. *Journal of Medical Education, 49,* 1040-1050.

Vernon, D. T. A., & Blake, R. L. (1993), Does problem-based learning work? A meta-analysis of evaluative research. *Academic Medicine, 68* (7), 550-563.

Wilkerson, L., & Gijselaers, W. H. (1996). *Bringing problem-based learning to higher education: Theory and practice.* San Francisco, CA: Jossey-Bass Publishers.

Yamane, D. (1996). Collaboration and its discontents: Steps toward overcoming barriers to successful group projects. *Teaching Sociology, 24,* 378-383.

Chapter Three

Horticulture; Planning and Landscape Architecture; and Sociology

Mary Taylor Haque, Lolly Tai, & Brenda Vander Mey

Abstract

A case study involving the creation of sustainable landscapes for a low-income community in Clemson, S.C. is used to illustrate the methodology and evaluation of a service learning project. Clemson University students enhanced their education in landscape design and implementation through a partnership with the City of Clemson, Habitat for Humanity, the National Wildlife Federation, and others which resulted in the creation of a certified backyard habitat for low income residents. Statistical pre and posttests reveal significant changes in the students' knowledge. These changes included knowing more about organizations that provide community service, greater accuracy with regard to native plants for upstate South Carolina, and components of wildlife habitats and planting procedures.

Service Learning Framework and Introduction

Community Service Learning (CSL) is a pedagogy of reflective inquiry linking students involvement in community service with their intellectual and moral development (Saltmarsh, 1996). Since the term "service learning" was coined in the late 1960's, this approach has found justification in educational institutions as both an alternative pedagogy and as a movement aimed at transforming the culture of American higher education (Saltmarsh, 1996; Barber, 1992; Barber & Battistoni, 1993; Kendall, 1990).

Why service learning? In *Rethinking Tradition*, Tamar Kupiec presents a rationale for integrating service and academic study. The educational benefit is perhaps the strongest argument for the inclusion of service learning in the curriculum. More effective teaching and learning, more effective serving, and more effective collaboration between campus and community are the three cornerstones for his rationale. (Kupiec, 1993). In addition, it has been noted that research now shows that service learning can help individuals not only develop substantive knowledge and practical skills, but also contributes to 'life-long social responsibility and civic values" (Checkoway, 1996, p. 600; see also Bringle and Hatcher, 1996).

Colleges and universities are reporting increasing numbers of courses and academic departments incorporating service learning. Combining community service with academic research, reading, writing and reflection can ensure that service enhances, and is enhanced by, the learning process (Miller, Steele, and Smith, 1995). McAleavey found that students frequently develop a sense of connectedness to their community through bonds forged with the client groups and colleagues at their service site. They also acquire a sense of "power", or importance, as they are recognized for their accomplishments. Many theorists and reformers are pointing to the need for higher education to become more relevant, more integrated, and more connected to the community (Bringle and Hatcher, 1996; Nyden et al., 1997). Similarly, the business world is calling on us to produce more well rounded individuals with relevant experience, good social skills, and creative thinking skills. Others are calling for educational reform that fosters environmental stewardship and the development of environmental stewards (Orr, 1995; Corson, 1995). Service learning can be a vehicle for such changes to happen (McAleavey, 1995). In addition, research shows that when compared to traditionally transmitted courses, service learning courses, when measured by mid-term and final examinations, had higher academic achievements (Bringle and Hatcher, 1996).

Many institutional partnerships have been created to enhance and disseminate information about service learning, a pedagogy still new on many campuses.   The Corporation for National Service provides funding assistance to help provide more services in the community and to institutionalize service on individual campuses.   Created by the National and Community Service Trust Act of 1993, the Corporation has increased national awareness of community service through its AmeriCorps, Learn and Serve America and national Senior Service Corps programs.   Learn and Serve grants provide funding for service learning programs that address local community needs in education, public safety, human services and the environment (Kobrin, Mareth, and Smith (ed.), 1996). Campus Compact, the Corporation for National Service, Learn and Serve America, and the Clemson University Service Learning Collaborative funded the following service learning project.

The Project

A case study utilizing service-learning and involving the creation of sustainable, learning landscapes for a low-income community in Clemson, S.C., is used to illustrate the methodology and evaluation of a service-learning project.   Due to the fact that many housing programs fund the construction of the home, but do not include funding or provisions for the surrounding landscapes, this project was intended to address the issue of enhancement of the open space around buildings as well as landscaping the properties surrounding homes in Red Hills Subdivision through a collaboration between Clemson University students and community partners.   Building on a recent strategic alliance formed between Habitat for Humanity International (HFHI) and the National Wildlife Federation (NWF), this project involved local partners of undergraduate horticulture and landscape architecture classes, City of Clemson officials, the Pickens County Habitat for Humanity chapter, elementary age at risk children enrolled in the "Sprouting Wings" program, the South Carolina Landscapes for Learning Collaborative, the South Carolina Wildlife Federation (an affiliate of NWF), low income home owners, volunteers, and faculty.

The aim was to research, design, and reflect on a sustainable and efficient landscape for five new homes for low-income families. Clemson students from several courses worked towards advancing their knowledge and commitment to environmental stewardship and enhanced their education through this partnership, which resulted in the implementation of a wildlife habitat garden for residents.

One goal of this project was to reach out to a more ethnically and culturally diverse population by assisting homeowners and volunteers in creating NWF certified backyard wildlife habitats on the home site and to promote sustainable community environments for low income families as well as for wildlife. Another goal was to provide an opportunity for students to learn and mature through participation in a project that has a long-term impact that is both visible and measurable. To that end, students and faculty from landscape architecture, sociology, and horticulture worked with homeowners, volunteers, and local officials in four phases. 1) Research, analysis, and information gathering; 2) planning and design; 3) scheduling and implementation, and 4) reflection, evaluation, sharing, and recognition.

Clemson third year landscape architecture students used their creative abilities and know-how to design alternative master plans for the Red Hill Subdivision. The project goal was to site five single-family homes of 1200 square feet each on a 1.7 acre site. The homes were to be accessed off a shared road terminating in a cul-de-sac. The primary objective was to accomplish this goal with minimal destruction to the site (vegetation and grading) while enhancing the environment through concepts of conservation. The designs generated followed a design process involving research, site inventory and analysis, design, construction drawings, cost estimating, implementation and documentation. The research, site inventory and analysis is critical to understanding the existing conditions and issues of the site and in setting project goals to accomplish the intended objectives.

Research

The research for the Red Hill Project focused on sustainability specific to the conservation and /or preservation for wildlife, water (xeriscape) and energy. Findings on wildlife preservation indicated that food, water, shelter, and safe places to raise young are essential elements to be integrated into the design. Thus, for example, fruit bearing plants for food; bird baths for water; trees and shrubs for shelter and a place to raise the young were significant to the design. Research on water conservation led to the concept of xeriscape or conservation through the use of seven principles including: 1) careful planning and design, 2) appropriate lawn areas, 3) thorough soil preparation, 4) appropriate use of plant materials, 5) effective and efficient watering methods, 6) use of mulch on trees, shrubs, and flower beds and 7) proper landscape maintenance. Following the xeriscape concept can successfully create lush landscapes vs. dry landscapes. Research on energy conservation revealed the importance of tree cover in reducing solar radiation and ultimately in power consumption. Carefully placed trees can save up to 25% in energy bills for heating and cooling. Deciduous trees added on the east and west sides of buildings block and absorb hot summer sun and allow the sun to warm the home in the winter. Trees also reduce the temperature by 3-6 degrees Fahrenheit as a result of evaporative cooling. Thus, basic principles including minimizing tree removal and destruction of tree roots and strategically planting new trees contribute to alleviating solar radiation.

Site Inventory and Analysis

A property boundary and topographic survey map was essential at the beginning of the project. Students conducted field work to determine on and off site opportunities and constraints and recorded it on the survey map. They documented and assessed the site and its size, the slope and drainage patterns, + 70' power right-of-way line, existing vegetation, views, noise, traffic, wind and sun orientation, structures, etc. They concluded that: 1) the site was tight for the number of homes; 2) a large portion of the site was unusable and/or difficult to build on due to the power line and steep slopes; 3) existing trees of 8 inches + caliper would need to be saved; 4) views, noise and traffic along the interstate highway would need to be buffered; and 5) the existing structure (under construction) would need to be integrated into the design.

Design

The students incorporated their research and site inventory and analysis into their conceptual designs. Various alternative drawings, including master plan, planting plan, grading plan and details were generated, displaying a broad range of design ideas. The common theme among the plans was to create a sustainable place with a sense of community. One student stated: "We tried to accomplish our goals by creating a natural corridor for wildlife and residents alike, . . . designing individual lots with specific interests of the users, considering such issues as privacy, recreation and certain plant species, . . . reducing the amount of paving to maintain the feel of the natural corridor along the community space".

Planting

The planting plan was designed with intentions of creating an aesthetic environment with seasonal interests that would attract wildlife, minimize solar radiation and incorporate principles of xeriscape and complement the overall design of the project. Thus, plants were used for the following purposes:

❖ berry, nut, seed, flower, and tender leaf bearing shrubs for attracting wildlife;
❖ evergreen shrubs and trees for screening and buffering;
❖ canopy trees for shading homes, parking areas, and the main road;
❖ small lawn and perennial bed areas for accent and proportion at the front of homes.

Grading

The grading plan is a technical drawing that must be designed and mathematically calculated to illustrate the manipulation of contours on the site to accommodate the project. The students worked diligently to find the best solution to balancing the cut and fill in the grading. In particular, they were challenged by factors of siting homes on steep terrain, maintaining grades around the roots of trees, incorporating retaining walls to minimize severe slope areas, etc. The final grading was kept to a minimum and the homes were integrated into the natural slope of the site. Gentle drainage swales carry water to the underground storm drainage system in the road. The road was graded to a rolling slope of 5% wherever possible for ease of driving conditions.

Cost Estimate and Implementation

With the completion of the design, the next phase of the project involved cost estimating, purchasing of plant materials, and coordination of labor, planting, tools, equipment, work days, etc. Several work days were scheduled and each group of students was assigned specific tasks. For example, the following teams were formulated: layout, staking, planting trees, shrubs, groundcovers, vines, and vegetables, watering, raking, mulching, etc. Students worked side by side with homeowners and community volunteers, and they gained a tremendous sense of pride at the completion of the implementation. Many students remarked that they looked forward to seeing the project mature.

Documentation

The overall design process was documented in the form of a brochure and a poster. The brochure consists of an introduction, project research, initial and final design phase and conclusion. Students were responsible for writing the text, producing the graphics and assembling the booklet with the use of Photoshop and Pagemaker computer graphics programs. A 24"x36" poster board also documents the project by summarizing and combining the project description, final master plan and various news articles.

Reports

The final plans, completed by students in Professor Lolly Tai's third year landscape architecture studio at Clemson University were presented to their client and invited critics. While Professor Lolly Tai's students worked on master planning, Professor Mary Haque's students developed planting plans and educational materials for the project. Students in Horticulture 304 designed perennial gardens with a wildlife theme. They visited Cane Creek Farm and Nursery to purchase plants for the project, and were involved in the installation of their designs. Students in Horticulture 208 developed educational handouts on landscape implementation and maintenance. Individual reports and early drafts were peer reviewed, and groups worked together to develop presentation quality final handouts. They met with homeowners to give them these reports and shared ideas on maintenance and care of the landscape in informal oral educational sessions on site.

Mr. Joshua Reed, an undergraduate horticulture student, spearheaded the implementation phase with Mr. Karl Muzii, a graduate horticulture student. Mr. Reed and Professors Haque, Tai, and Vander Mey reported project results at the International Meeting of the American Society of Horticultural Science in Charlotte, N.C. in 1998. Professors Haque, Tai, and Vander Mey are finalizing a refereed journal article for submission to HortTechnology. Two abstracts have already been published in Hort Science.

Planned and Unplanned Outcomes

The project resulted in both student learning and community enhancement. In addition, the project was recognized for a 1998 Housing Achievement Award by the South Carolina Housing Finance and Development Authority. One home was the first Habitat for Humanity home to be registered and certified as a Backyard Wildlife Habitat by the National Wildlife Federation. The habitat partners received a 1998 Conservation Award in the organization category from the South Carolina Wildlife Federation. The project was featured on the National Wildlife Federation's web page, published in eight popular press articles, presented at the 1998 SC Environmental Conference in a poster session and featured on cable TV and in a video on service learning being produced for national distribution.

Evaluation of the Habitat Project: Knowledge Base Changes and Effects of Service Learning

While students from several classes worked on this project, the focus of the pre and post test evaluation will be on students enrolled in Horticulture 208, a three hour landscape appreciation course without a lab. The students in this class contributed an estimated total of 459 hours on this service-learning project. The individual low was one hour, the individual high 40 hours, with an average of 12.4 hours per student (standard deviation 7.26). Landscape architecture students contributed an estimated 2500 hours on studio design and implementation time.

Students enrolled in Landscape Appreciation (Hort. 208) were administered a pre test. Students did not receive a grade on this test. Background information obtained from students included their major, past work experience in horticulture, experience with landscape implementation or maintenance, past community volunteer work, and previous involvement in service learning projects.

Students were asked to identify Habitat for Humanity, The South Carolina Wildlife Federation, The National Wildlife Federation Backyard Habitat Program, and Campus Compact and were asked to indicate whether they had worked with any of these entities. Students then were asked to list 10 services that the City of Clemson provided its citizens. Students also were asked to define service learning. Knowledge needed for this specific project also was inventoried. Students were asked to identify the four critical components needed in a design intended to attract wildlife, to list 10 native plants that would be appropriate for use in a residential yard or garden in the Clemson area, and to describe the planting process for a flower bed in Clemson, South Carolina where the soils consist primarily of heavy red clay.

Students were asked to provide all of the information indicated above, excluding background information, in the posttest at the conclusion of the semester. Unlike the pretest, however, the posttest was graded as part of the final examination for the course. Thirty-six students completed both the pre and posttests.

Background Information on Participating Students

Of the 36 students completing both the pre and posttests, 66.7% were majoring in horticulture, 27.8% were majoring in some other area of agriculture or plant science, and the remaining 5.6% were "other" majors. While most (88.9%) had volunteered in their communities, very few (8.3%) had ever engaged in Service Learning.

In the pre test, most students had heard of Habitat for Humanity, and most could adequately describe The National Wildlife Federation Backyard Wildlife Habitat Program and The South Carolina Wildlife Federation (usually just indicated that these groups promoted the protection of wildlife). In addition, most students gave a passable, albeit general, definition of Service Learning. However, most students had no idea what Campus Compact, the funding agency, was.

Background information on the students rendered these vague definitions understandable. Only 13.9% had ever worked with Habitat for Humanity. Very few of the students had worked with either the South Carolina Wildlife Federation (5.6%) or the National Wildlife Federation Backyard Wildlife Habitat Program (2.8%). No students had experience related to Campus Compact.

Changes in Student Knowledge, Pre and Post

T tests identified significant changes in student knowledge from the beginning to end of the semester. At the pretest, the mean number of organizations identified (out of a possible 4) was 1.53. At the posttest, the mean was 3.25. At the pretest, the mean number of correctly identified planting components (out of 3 considered essential) was 1.31. The posttest revealed a mean of 2.2 on the same item. City services identification improved greatly from the pre to the post test. Native plant identification also improved, though not as dramatically. Finally, and quite notably, students' ability to identify the 4 components of a wildlife habitat went from a mean of 2.11 at the pretest to a perfect 4.0 at the posttest.

The only item that revealed no significant change pre and post was the students' ability to adequately define Service Learning. Written comments made on the pretest revealed that while most students had not engaged in Service Learning, they had heard about it.

Effects of Service Learning

During the posttest, students were asked how many service learning hours they had put in on the Habitat Project, whether because of the project they are less, equally or more likely to engage in volunteer projects in the future, and how much more conscious (not really, somewhat, yes more, yes very much more) they were of organizations that provide opportunities for community service and volunteerism. They also were asked to rate the degree to which Service Learning had been a helpful work experience for them (no, not at all; yes, somewhat; yes, adequately/well).

Almost three-fourths (71%) of the students said that because of this Habitat project, they are likely to very likely to engage in more service activities. Well over half of the students (63%) said that because of this project they are more conscious of organizations and institutions that provide service/volunteerism opportunities; 14% said that they were "very much so" more conscious.

Pearson's correlation tests were conducted to discern any correlation among and between these items. There were positive and significant ($p=.05$) correlation between increased consciousness of organizations providing service and volunteerism opportunities and hours served on the Habitat project ($r=.357$); consciousness and willingness to be involved in more Service-Learning project ($r=.418$); and, rating this Service Learning project as a helpful work experience ($r=.418$).

The Project's Interface With Student Work Experience

Students were asked whether this Habitat project provided them with a helpful work experience. Almost half (46%) of the students responding said that the project had provided them well or adequately with a helpful work experience, 40% rated the project as somewhat helpful, and 14% of the students rated the project as not at all helpful as a work experience.

Implications of this Evaluation

The statistical tests reveal significant changes in the students' knowledge. These changes included knowing more about organizations that provide community service and volunteerism opportunities, knowing more about what services one city provides its citizens, and greater accuracy with regard to native plants for a specific area and components of wildlife habitats and planting procedures. It is reasonable to assert that these documented changes were a result of involvement in the Habitat project. Thus, one can conclude that this project helped facilitate learning for the students involved.

Correlation analysis revealed significant and positive relationships between increased consciousness of organizations providing volunteer opportunities and number of hours spent on the Habitat project, an increased likeliness of volunteering in the future, and agreeing that this Service Learning project had been helpful to the students. Finally, most students saw this project as either helpful or very helpful to them as a work experience.

While future projects also must engender this type of follow up documentation, based upon the findings from the evaluation of the current project, one may tentatively conclude that hands-on Service Learning provides a constructive approach to knowledge based enhancement and more positive attitudes toward volunteerism and community service.

Benefits and Challenges of Service Learning

Service learning needs to consider the personal and intellectual growth of both the student and the community. "The goal is to help students constantly critique, evaluate and build on knowledge and move to intellectually 'higher ground' and, at the same time, continue to critically examine their roles within our complex and diverse society." (Cone and Harris, 1996 p.41). Compelling insights often emerge in student reaction papers written during the reflection and evaluation phase of projects. The following quotations from students working on the habitat project illustrate a few discoveries made by students as a result of service learning.

Being able to put in the vegetable garden after spending time researching the vegetables and planting was very valuable. I found that I learned more by having a hands on experience with this that if I had been sitting in a class listening to a lecture about it. Much to my surprise as well, I enjoyed going out and getting my hands dirty. I also think that it will be really neat to drive by the house and think that I had something to do with it looking that great.

While this student benefited most from the combination of library research and hands on planting, another student learned more through teaching others:

...I helped plant some of the materials in the yard. However, I found that I learned more at the Earth Day Celebration. I had the chance to explain the design and why we choose to do things the way we did.

Yet another student learned more about team work as a result of the project:

I certainly know more than I did about planting trees, establishing vegetable and herb gardens, and turf than I would have imagined. Actually doing hands-on work with plants is a great teacher. The group involvement was also very educational! I liked planting the vegetables best!

Students with previous experience enjoy the leadership opportunities associated with service learning:

> My father owns a nursery so I have had experience implementing landscapes. I did, however, gain experience through organizing a group to perform a task. (Usually my dad gives all the orders!)

Others with little experience learn basic information while expanding their outlook and attitudes:

> For one, I learned what a groundcover is. Like I said in my reaction paper though, I probably learned more about my attitude towards service and the difference that volunteering can make than I learned about horticulture.

While personal and social growth are valuable benefits of service learning, technical information related to the discipline and course are considered integral to the process:

> Yes, I learned the best locations to plant specific trees and shrubs. I learned about grading, runoff, and water conservation in regard to designing a landscape.

We faced two major challenges on this service learning project. The first was the challenge of scheduling the outdoor portion of the project, which involved landscape implementation. Construction and rain repeatedly delayed the implementation, so we had to be flexible, and students, faculty, and clients were forced to practice character development in the areas of patience and perseverance. The second major challenge was learning to deal with incompetence. Students worked hard on their designs developing grading plans which preserved existing vegetation on-site, and everyone was disappointed when the graders bulldozed the site in an incompetent manner which resulted in serious erosion problems, water running into the basement of the home, and loss of trees and wildlife habitat. One student wrote: "I enjoyed 'lending a helping hand' at the Habitat for Humanity house. It was a lot of fun just go get out there with my fellow classmates and work towards a common goal. I had little trouble knowing what materials went where. But I did learn about incompetancies of so-called professionals who do poor work. I learned first hand how you really have a lot of headaches when you deal with people such as graders, electricians, etc. if they don't do their jobs properly the first time around." Having to deal with incompetence and mistakes will hopefully impress upon students the importance of acquiring skills and responsibility.

The selection of real world projects for landscape design classes can greatly influence student motivation and learning while simultaneously helping solve community problems. This project encouraged creative thinking and problem solving and taught students more about client relationships, presentation techniques, and actual design with the land.

Working with town planners, land owners, and public service organizations quickly gave students a feeling for how cities and towns are governed. An appreciation of the need for community involvement is also learned. Perhaps the most important lesson landscape architects, sociologists, and horticultural scientists can learn is that a good plan grows from the site and from the needs of the people, plants, and wildlife that inhabit that site. It should not be designed in a studio to be imposed on the land; it should seem a natural outgrowth of the site and should preserve and enhance the best features of the community.

Students learned some hard "real world" lessons about how difficult it is to schedule projects; they got to practice character traits of patience and perseverance as they experienced project delays and rainy weather. They gained an understanding of how quickly nature and natural sites can be destroyed through poor grading and development. As a result, they understand the importance of tree protection and sedimentation control on project sites. They gained experience working with clients and had several opportunities to practice presentation techniques and perfect oral communication skills. After learning how to complete a plan that is environmentally, functionally and aesthetically sound, students shared their ideas and educated others.

Summary and Conclusion

In conclusion, Clemson University and the Clemson community partnered with national and state organizations, communicated, and worked toward common goals to the benefit of all. This project provided a network through which college students could engage in hands-on, practical environmental education, environmental stewardship, and public service while also providing a network to assist community members in enhancing their environments.   Building community relationships and providing environmental education by integrating teaching, research and service allowed students and professors to expand and grow. In the words of an undergraduate horticulture student who worked on the project: "Service learning is a win/win situation for the community, the university, and the students." As an innovative and unique project addressing many neighborhood, community, environmental , and educational issues, this project has become a service-learning model. This prototype is being adapted by Habitat for Humanity International and the National Wildlife Federation to launch their new alliance at the national level as they prepare a "Tool Kit" to distribute to affiliates across the country.

Works Cited

Barber, B. (1992). *An aristocracy of everyone: The politics of education and the future of America.* Oxford: Oxford University Press.

Barber, B. & Battistoni, R. (1993). A season of service: Introducing service learning into the liberal arts curriculum. *PS: Political Science and Politics, June: 235-262.*

Bringle, R. G. and J. A. Hatcher. (1996). Implementing service learning in higher education. *Journal of Higher Education. Vol. 67, 221-240.*

Checkaway, B. (1996). Combining service and learning on campus and in the community. *Phi Delta Kappan, Vol. 77, 600-606.*

Cone, D. and S. Harris. (1996).   Service-learning practice: developing a theoretical framework. *Michigan Journal of Community Service Learning. Vol. 3, 31-41.*

Corson, W. H. (1995). Priorities for a sustainable future: the role of education, the media, and tax reform. *Journal of Social Issues, Vol. 51, 37-61.*

Greenleaf, R.K. (1977). *Servant leadership.* New York/Mahwah: Paulist Press.

Kendall, J. & Associates. (1990). *Combining service and learning: A resource book for community and public service, Volumes 1 and 2.* Raleigh, N.C.: National Society for Internships and Experiential Education.

Kobrin, M, and J. Mareth, M. Smith, Editor. (1996). *Service matters A sourcebook for community service in higher education.* Campus Compact/The Education Commission of the States.

Kupiec, T. Y. (1993). *Rethinking tradition: Integrating service with academic study on college campuses.* Published by Campus Compact/The Education Commission of the States.

McAleavey, S. (1995). *A theory of human behavior and service learning. Service counts: Lessons from the field of service and higher education.* Campus Compact/The Education Commission of the States.

Miller, M. and L. Steele, M. Smith, (ed.) (1995). *Service counts: Lessons from the field of service and higher education.* Campus Compact/The Education Commission of the States.

Nyden, P., A. Figert, M. Shibley and D. Burrows. (1997). University-community collaborative research: adding chairs at the research table. In Nyden, P., A. Figert, M. Shibley and D. Burrows, eds., *Building Community: Social Science in Action.* Thousand Oaks, CA: Pine Forge Press. 3-13.

Orr, D. W. (1995). Educating for the environment: Higher education's challenge of the next century. *Change, Vol. 27, 43-47.*

Saltmarsh, J. (1996). Education for critical citizenship: John Dewey's contribution to the pedagogy of community service learning. *Michigan Journal of Community Service Learning. Vol. 3, 13-21.*

Chapter Four

Public Health and Parks, Recreation & Tourism

Jennifer Hinton, Francis McGuire, Judith Witthoeft, Jessyna McDonald, & Deb Mitchell

The Project

Three faculty and three students from a combination of the departments of Public Health and Parks, Recreation, and Tourism Management came together in the fall of 1998 to create a course that integrated service learning with health principles education. The team chose the course "Health Promotion for the Aged" for its capability to take on the project. The course focused on the analysis and evaluation of health related problems of the aged. Emphasis was on the concepts of positive health behaviors and understanding the multidimensional aspects of aging.

One section of the course offered an additional credit hour in which the service project was carried out, while the other section served as the control group. The project team met numerous times in grant development. A grant for student travel was secured through the Dropout Prevention Center at Clemson University. Also a large grant was received from the Corporation for National Service through the University of Pittsburgh.

The service learning project incorporated into the Health Promotion for the Aged class focused on creating cadres containing both older adults and students who worked to carry out the service learning action plans. The project had three primary goals: 1) Assist traditional university students and older persons in learning concepts of health; 2) Provide these two cadres with the opportunity to interact in a service program and establish reality-based perceptions of each other; and 3) Provide a service to the communities participating as service learning sites.

Properly delivering this service included understanding the barriers associated with the implementation of identified needs in each project, and evaluating the effectiveness of the plans carried out at each site. Five sites agreed to collaborate on meeting the education and service needs of the course. These sites included a long-term care facility, a continuing care community, a retirement community, a multipurpose senior center, and a church. Prior to the semester, the project team met with primary leaders at each of the sites to discuss the project, to determine each site's interest areas, and to become better acquainted with each leader and the needs of the facilities they represented.

Service Learning Framework

Preparation

The first meetings between the students and older adults included pre-testing on two attitude scales, project overviews, an informative lecture, and collaboration to begin needs assessments at each of the sites. The students broke into groups dependent upon their interests that complemented the sites already established. Each cadre of older and younger adults had a University mentor (project team faculty or graduate student) to help facilitate the service learning process.

Each cadre conducted informal needs assessments and created plans for project implementation at each of the sites. The planning and research done by students was based on needs assessment results, and was included in the description of action for each site and the respective project. Students did not write formal proposals, but rather all decisions were made along with the older adults in each cadre group. Decisions and projects were monitored by each group's university contact, the class instructor, and the project coordinator.

Action

As each group was unique, so were their contributions over the semester. These projects varied widely in subject matter and scope, but all could be considered part of the course objectives in the area of health and aging. Each of the 28 students was required to put forty-five hours into the project, but many put in closer to 60 out-of-class hours. As a group, they contributed over 1260 hours to the community! Each individual cadre's project is discussed separately in the pages to follow.

Long-Term Care Facility

The cadre at the long-term care facility chose to complete projects in the areas of horticulture therapy and pet therapy. They chose this area because of the current research and interest regarding the Eden Alternative. The Eden Alternative is a template for facilities in which older adults reside that attempts to make the facility more home-like, to make activities stimulating and continually accessible to the residents, and to make the environment conducive to assisting residents to be more independent in their choices. The students were attempting to incorporate aspects similar to parts of the Eden Alternative into this particular facility. This facility has a modern approach to care for older adults wherein rooms are already made to be "homey" and residents are encouraged to be as independent as possible.

One activity this cadre offered was pet therapy. The students learned that health regulations in this area are quite strict, which limited the scope of their originally intended program. They finally settled on using one dog for pet therapy at the facility, and monitored the success of the dog in creating attitude enhancement. The students also undertook the planting of a garden with the residents.

Continuing Care Facility

The cadre at this site identified the problem of poor nutrition for some of the older adults who live alone, and decided that their focus would be nutrition counseling. The cadre met approximately once a week. They discussed nutritional principles and the difficulties in cooking for one person. The cadre created a meal together, and developed a cookbook with a variety of recipes focused on smaller meals for people who lived alone. This cookbook was printed and distributed to the residents in this community. Nutritional guidelines and needs for older adults were studied by this group. They focused on finding the barriers of older adults who live alone in meeting necessary nutritional requirements.

Retirement Community without Health Care Services

The cadre at this site was very large, and included several people from the older adult community involved. The older adults began the project with a debate already raging about including health options in their community. This debate had begun due to the limited scope of both private and public agencies supplying non-emergency health care. The residents felt that their money was not well spent on some available health and other services (such as home maintenance). Many of the health services available often did not include any quality of life needs but rather only those deemed absolutely medically necessary.

Several focus groups met to discern a direction for action. Since there were two vocal, opposing positions, the focus often changed between meetings. Finally, a decision was made to create two separate intergenerational teams. One team was to inventory public and private resources. The other was to bring the issue of the "Care Initiative" to all of the residents in the establishment.

The latter cadre decided to create and disperse a survey to obtain input from all the residents of the community. The survey asked questions about current and future health care options, and each resident's choice to input money for a resource coordinator to facilitate these options. The initiative was to find what was necessary, and acceptable, to the community to enable residents to stay in their homes as their health level declined.

The second team completed a market analysis of health care and other services available for older adults in the surrounding communities. They created a large resource guide that was printed and distributed to residents. The residents of the community have put this guide on the internet, and continually update it as new information becomes available.

Methods of survey design were intensively studied within this group. They also learned specific methods for leading focus groups effectively. Conflict resolution skills were heavily practiced in this situation, due to the volatility of the group on the issue at hand.

Community Senior Center

The senior center was one of the more challenging sites in the project. The focus of the cadre was continually changing. The first attempt at focusing the project was in the area of marketing the Center so that more older adults in the community could gain wellness benefits through usage, and so that the financial base of the center would increase. However, many of the older adults involved at the Center were not interested in increasing their membership, and the initiative changed to involving current members to a greater extent.

A concurrent goal brought to the cadre was that of improving the meals currently served at lunch hour. However, after looking into other options, the older adults decided that the meals were improving and that this was not an appropriate goal.

The students returned to their initial marketing effort, and began to investigate additional sources of funding that did not increase membership as had been discussed earlier. The students also looked into several other areas. They investigated internet access, a membership interest assessment, updating the computer at the center so as to be able to print their own newsletter, and a resource center containing health information. However, none of these actions ever came to fruition. The barriers will be discussed later in the chapter.

Community Church

This cadre decided upon a project whose main focus would be physical health. They dubbed the program "FITSPAN", from a similar program created by Dr. Jessyna McDonald for use with other African American churches. FITSPAN stands for Fitness, Intergenerational Teamwork, Spirituality, Physical Activity, and Nutrition. The students decided to modify the original program in an effort to better meet the needs of the group involved. The cadre set up the church members' fitness group so that each older adult participating would have a child or young adult partner who also participated.

This group of students applied learned principles of exercise physiology. They intensively studied elements of proper warm-up, stretching, and cardiovascular exercise for older adults. They studied injury prevention and motivational techniques to get group members to participate, and continue with their participation.

The initial program ran for six weeks, with a follow-up leader being elected from the church to keep it running. Each class began with a prayer and scripture reading given by a church member, followed by a segment on health promotion prepared by one of the university students, and finally a thirty-minute exercise session. The church cafeteria was the site for the exercise sessions, designed by the students to improve muscle strength, cardiovascular function, and flexibility. All exercises used a chair for balance or sitting.

Reflection

Each cadre decided on their meeting frequency as they felt necessary. In meetings, they had the opportunity to discuss and receive feedback from their project coordinator (one of the original faculty/ graduate student team members). The course instructor also fielded questions in class on a regular basis, and the health student who was the project coordinator held a number of informal discussions throughout the semester. Groups also discussed items over e-mail at different intervals. Students also got feedback from the participating older adults by other means.

For example, the cadre who completed the pet therapy project created a ranking form. A student would observe the pet therapy interactions with the residents, and complete the form based on their perceptions of the interaction. The form contained nine (9) actions that the older adult may take toward the pet, including such items as talks to pet, strokes pet, watches pet, and smiles at pet. They discussed these observations with one another and reflected on the salience of the method.

At the end of the course, each student was required to write a reflection paper. These papers were to include the benefits of the project, as well as the barriers and the students' personal feelings about the project. Each student group was also required to prepare a formal presentation. This presentation was completed at a Saturday workshop that hosted all of the cadres including the students, older adults, and project advisors. Many of the students commented that this time period was extremely beneficial in that their sharing led to a more thorough understanding and integration of the learning that took place. The students who worked with the FITSPAN project seemed to feel especially successful. Two of the three young women who worked with this group volunteered to speak at a presentation concerning the Health Promotion for the Aged class over six months after the course was completed. They were very articulate in discussing their challenges, fears, and successes. They seemed especially pleased with the relationships they created with the church members, and the lack of racial barriers they felt they had experienced. Both women discussed their increased confidence in their ability to complete their tasks as they moved into the work force as health educators.

Celebration

Time limitations of the semester also limited some of the individual group celebrations. Some groups did create celebratory products, such as FITSPAN T-shirts for the exercisers. The meal prepared at the end of the nutrition group was also considered a final celebration, and cookbooks were printed to be distributed as well. The final celebration was during the Saturday workshop at the end of the semester. Both students and older adults in each of the five cadres had the opportunity to "show off" their accomplishments, and to share their struggles along the way. Final deliverable products and photos were set on display. A luncheon allowed people to informally spend time in closure with one another.

Planned and Unplanned Outcomes

Student data from the two attitude pre- and post-tests were examined. The first was a semantic differential scale about perceptions of older adults. It contained a total of 20 pairs of items that students rated on a seven-point scale. The second was a 20 item questionnaire that asked students to agree or disagree with statements about older adults on a five-point scale. The pre- and post test scores were compared for the group who did the additional service learning hours and for the control group--another section of the class.

Using an ANCOVA that removed the influence of pre-test differences between the groups, it was found that post-test scores of the two groups were significantly different on both scales. For scale one, there was a mean difference of 15.680 points between the treatment and control groups (p = .005). Eleven items changed significantly for the treatment group when viewed independently, and all 20 items moved in a positive direction. For scale two, there was also a significant mean difference (p = .014) of 3.784. The service learning group scored more positively than the control group. Though the pretest was significant in both scales in that better pre-test scores predicted better post-test scores, those effects did not eliminate the significantly higher gains of the group who had service learning experiences on both attitude tests.

Additionally, students stated that they liked the service learning component, and felt they'd gained from it (more than from traditional experience). They noted their self-confidence, their ability to adapt to the needs of the participants, and their increased skill in working with people different from themselves as attributes they didn't feel they would have gained in the classroom. They also specifically discussed how salient a "real" experience was, as opposed to contrived classroom assignments where they felt they were always "pretending".

Good things came about for some of the facilities in which the students worked as well. A local middle school is continuing the pet therapy program at the continuing care facility. The retirement community has gained approval from its citizens to hire a resource director, and is looking into the ways in which to achieve this goal. Three more churches have voiced a desire to participate in the FITSPAN project, and are working on creating similar programs and searching for appropriate leadership.

Challenges

Developing a plan that includes all faculty and community members at the beginning of the project is essential. It was found that it was good to meet with all of the older adults on "neutral ground" to discuss project options and to get everyone set before the beginning of the semester. Although this was attempted, there were still unanswered questions before the students began meeting with the older adults to begin needs assessment and planning. Due to this, all sites were not clear about the purpose/ intent of the service learning process. There were times that the lack of more intensive discussion at the beginning of the program became a detriment, as the students and older adults sometimes had different ideas of what the service learning was to accomplish.

Timing was the major issue of the project. The course took an extraordinary amount of planning to coordinate five different community sites with five different university leaders in two academic departments. The student who served as project coordinator was absolutely essential in this sense. She was the best cog in the wheel to move messages through the course instructor and the other students. Despite this, there continued to be a difficulty with communication and keeping all leaders and students in the same feedback group. More involvement in the classroom by the non-departmental leaders may have helped to alleviate some of this difficulty. It may have also left some more time for covering other essential classroom material, which Dr. Witthoeft, the primary instructor, says was challenging due to the students' heavy interest and involvement in the out of class projects.

Also related to timing was the difficulty of the students and older adults coordinating their hours to meet. Students have strict class and work schedules that often take up their daytime hours. This is also the time that most older adults prefer to work on projects. This was often due to other commitments they had. In some cases the hours of the facility are limited, meal times are limiting, and many of the older adults preferred not to drive in the nighttime hours. Many students had difficulty in fitting their schedules with the others in their cadre. At times this was exacerbated by long drives to get to some of the sites, which varied from ten minutes to forty-five minutes.

Only minimal resistance of the students and the older adults toward one another was encountered. However, it is important to be aware of this barrier. Some students felt that the older adults might not accept them, and were apprehensive in beginning their projects and sharing their ideas. A couple of students admitted feeling very self-conscious as the projects began, and feeling extremely relieved when their older adult partners "welcomed us with open arms".

On the other hand, some of the older adult leaders admitted there were persons in their group who, as professionals, felt that the students were not experienced enough to bring expertise to the cadre; these participants had negative attitudes toward that "irresponsible, pot-smoking bunch of kids". One person in particular stated that despite these shortcomings, he felt that they were blessed with a good group of "dedicated, challenging young people who persevered throughout the project".

As one can see, these barriers can be overcome. It takes continual encouragement and persistence of the project directors to facilitate growth between the generations. Many of the project directors also felt that many barriers were broken down by the older adult project leaders who were part of the original planning. They seemed to work as liaisons between the students and the other older adults involved in the project, providing both a buffer and a bridge to link the two generations.

There were other issues that also created kinks in the plans. Students learned that agencies are highly regulated, and budgetary and health guidelines that seem elementary can squelch even the best thought out ideas. They found that plants die unexpectedly, and that sometimes people really do not want to be part of what they consider a wonderful program! Some groups found that projects change frequently due to restrictions, leaders' schedules, and politics. They also learned many conflict resolution and communication skills while working through these difficulties.

Summary and Conclusion

The intergenerational service learning projects completed in Health Promotion for the Aged was truly a learning experience not only for students, but for faculty and older adults as well. It provided opportunities for learning between and among young and older adults. It also strengthened ties between the University and community. It provided opportunities to generate new bonds of appreciation and understanding between young and old. In an era when the aging population is dramatically increasing, projects such as this will continue to assist in the promotion of healthy aging, a key component of successful relationships for generations to come.

Chapter Five

Marketing

Patricia A. Knowles

I have taught a Nonprofit Marketing course since the early 90s. Nonprofit marketing has to do with applying concepts of marketing such as exchange, consumer decision making, market research, and product, price, place, and promotion to public and private organizations that do not necessarily operate in order to make a profit. These organizations are sometimes referred to as social organizations and/or not-for-profit organizations and include all organizations classified under the 501(c)3 code of the Internal Revenue Service. Specific examples of such organizations are state park systems, educational and religious organizations, and organizations such as the Humane Society of the United States and the American Red Cross.

There are many ways to go about teaching such a class and, over the years, I have tried several. Of course, one could simply lecture, but in such a class the course material easily lends itself to direct application. At first, I had students choose nonprofit organizations in which they were interested and had them complete about six assignments applying course material to that nonprofit. While interesting to all, at times the classes become, perhaps, too interesting. I recall classes where I felt more like a referee than a professor, directing discussion between a

"NOW" student and an "NRA" student with seemingly everyone arguing with the "ACLU" student. More important, the six assignments completed by each student for his/her chosen nonprofit organization honestly did not help the nonprofit very much although that had been an intention on my part.

Searching for a less controversial way to involve students in the course material, I had the idea to have the entire class apply knowledge they learned in the class to only one nonprofit organization. This choice allows me to contact the nonprofit organization prior to the beginning of the course, explain the project the class would do for them, and request and receive materials from them (e.g., Financial and Annual Reports) that help the students complete their assignments. Furthermore, since the entire class is involved in the application project, more assignments can be completed for the nonprofit and, at the end of the semester, the class is able to complete enough assignments so that I can compile a 100+ page "Marketing Analysis" for the nonprofit. The project helps everyone including the nonprofit, the students, and even me.

The project allows me to address the four components of service learning – preparation, action, reflection, and recognition – which I will address in later sections of this chapter. It also allows me to get my students intimately involved in helping a real organization that really needs their help. After the first assignment, the students begin to understand the world of a nonprofit manager who must make decisions with little or no information. And, in fact, the students come to gain confidence in their own skills and abilities since they usually find that they know more about marketing than the people in the nonprofit with whom we work.

The Project

On the first day of class, I introduce students to the fact that we will be doing a Marketing Analysis for a nonprofit organization. The nonprofit for this particular project was a chapter of the American Red Cross but almost any nonprofit organization can benefit from such a project. I also explain that the "real-world" cost of a Marketing Analysis such as the one the class will do during the semester ranges from about $5,000 to $10,000 and is a fairly extensive undertaking. I explain my rationale for having them do the project. First, I, personally, want to do something for the community in which I live. And, being a professor at a university with includes a "service" component as part of its mission, helping people and organizations in my state fits with my university's mission. Second, I believe that students must learn how to apply what they have learned; that it is not enough for them to learn abstract facts. We know from other disciplines that unless students practice retrieval of information it is likely that the information will never again be used after appearing as answers on exams. So, in order to make the information they learn in the class more real to them, I include this application assignment as part of their course requirements. After the requisite moans and groans, the class, as a whole, seems pleased that they will be helping an organization – albeit a bit cautious about what is expected of them. Motivation is further stimulated when I inform them that they will be competing for order of authorship on the final document. That is, each student's name will actually appear on the title page of the final document with the only exceptions being those students that do not achieve an average "C" grade on their assignments. Also, students that receive at least a "C" on an individual assignment are noted immediately at the end of that assignment within the body of the report. Thus, students are motivated to perform well so that their names will appear on the document. Further they are motivated to work hard in order to out-perform others in terms of the quality of their applications since the order of authorship on the report is determined by overall scores on all six assignments.

Students are required to purchase a Course Booklet for the course in addition to their textbook and other materials. The Course Booklet for the application assignment includes a detailed explanation of the application assignment, all of the individual assignments from which they will be asked to choose six to complete, the most recent Annual Report (and any other information the nonprofit cares to provide), and a Marketing Analysis completed by a previous class for a different nonprofit organization. Of course, in the very first class where a Marketing Analysis was completed, I was not able to provide an already completed document. In that case, I was very specific about what I was looking for in each assignment.

Preparation

After the initial introduction to the course and the project, we spend about 3 to 3 1/2 weeks preparing for the beginning of the project. During that time, I introduce them to the specific nonprofit organization and I introduce them to the concept of nonprofit organizations in general. We often have one or two days of confusion as we sort out what is meant by public and private nonprofits (e.g., public nonprofits are supported by tax monies and private nonprofits rely on donations and volunteers) and how nonprofits are similar to and different from for-profit (a.k.a. business) firms. Until we get these very basic concepts straightened out, there is simply no point in having them try to apply information.

Action

Sometime during the first 3 weeks, we go over the first set of assignments in class. I go over each assignment in detail explaining what I will be looking for from them in their applications. I do not, however, direct them to any specific sources and allude to any answers, since, as I emphasize to them repeatedly, the analysis has not yet been done. That means that I do not have any answers and that they have to find them. In every case, students are directed to support or justify their applications. That is, they should not just tell me what they believe is the answer to the question, but they must carefully explain why they believe that and what evidence supports their answers. After I go over all the assignments in class, each student chooses three that they would prefer to work on and I assign one of their choices to each student. This results in about 3-6 students being assigned to each choice. Although instructors could then assign that small group to complete the assignment, I prefer that students work alone on their assignments so as to increase the amount and variety of answers. If they were to work in groups, while that may be easier for me to grade, it would reduce variability in the answers and reduce the quality of the overall document.

An example of an assignment from the first set of assignments is this: "How does being in the competitive/market stage help and hurt this chapter of the American Red Cross (ARC)? Your answer should include a very brief description of the four stages of evolution of nonprofits, a determination of the stage under which this chapter of the

ARC was 'born,' a way that being in the competitive/market stage helps and a way that being in the competitive/market stage hurts this chapter of the ARC." Students get the information that they need to understand what is being asked in the question from course lectures and their textbook. But, the information that they need to actually answer the question comes from sources only limited by their creativity. They are encouraged to search the internet, the library, and ask questions of me and people at the ARC chapter who have agreed to help. Of course, since the question has never been answered before, they have to think, reason, and apply their own knowledge.

At this point of the project, things usually get a bit tense in the classroom. As the deadline for submission of their first assignment comes ever closer, some students balk and at times I feel physically drained from the amount of encouragement I must do. But, I feel that it is my responsibility to pull them along, encourage them, and be their cheerleader at this stage. For many students, this is the first time they have ever had to complete an assignment for which there is not necessarily a correct answer. This seems especially troublesome for students with higher GPAs in that they are used to knowing the "right" answer and seem to feel especially uncomfortable when they are dealing in the especially muddied waters of the real world of a nonprofit manager. So, I must encourage them to faithfully step off into the space of the unknown and assure them that they will be supported.

One way I reduce tension in the classroom is to allow them to hand in assignments – before they are due – for me to look over. While I do not "pregrade" the assignments, I do take the opportunity to pull out my red pen and make comments directing them to other sources or crossing out whole sections that are not pertinent to the assignment at all. Although students do not like to receive a marked-up paper at this point, they usually agree that its much better to find out that they made mistakes or that they are totally on the wrong track at this stage rather than when the assignment is graded. In order to avoid the overwhelming situation of having to look over 30-35 assignments on the day an assignment is due, students are informed in their Course Booklet that I will not look over any assignment for any reason on the same day that one is due and I stand by my words on that issue.

Reflection

Once assignments are due, I try to grade them within one week. Each assignment is worth 20 points and when grading, I carefully explain why points were deleted from the overall score. This part comes as a shock to some students who seem to believe that because there is no written answer that already exists, there can be no way to lose points. However, although I emphasize often that students must justify their work, many simply do not. Thus, they lose points because they make unsupported statements. Or, they lose points because they misapply concepts from marketing, showing that they really do not (yet) understand them.

Regardless of what points they receive, all students are given the opportunity to re-write their assignments. They do this to 1) improve their grade in the class and on the assignments, and 2) to have a second chance to apply their knowledge appropriately for the final report which is only as good as are the assignments. In class, I go over any problems that seem to be pertinent to the whole class, e.g., if students completing one of the assignments consistently misapplied a major concept. I also take opportunities to note especially good work on assignments, bringing that to the attention of the entire class.

At this point, I combine the 3-6 students' assignments that made up one assignment into a coherent answer to a question. Students are identified for their contribution in order of the quality of their work on their subsection. As larger sections are completed, I make them available to the class so that everyone can see the Marketing Analysis take shape.

Recognition

Students receive recognition of their work through seeing the completed analysis –- with their names on it. In the semester that we completed the analysis for the ARC, everyone was able, because of our grant monies, to receive a free copy of the final Marketing Analysis. Watching students receive their copies is fun for me because I watch their eyes light up as they see their name on the front cover of the report (it doesn't seem to matter at this point if they were first or last) and also as they search inside the report for their name on individual assignments.

Once I have presented the Marketing Analysis to the nonprofit, students will often check in – some from jobs that they have taken – asking how the report was received and if I've heard anything about whether the report was useful. The point is that the students seem to take ownership of their work and are proud of it. For many, this is the first project they have done that ends up not in a professor's file drawer, but on the desk of a manager who may use it.

Outcomes and Evaluation

There were several planned outcomes of this project. First, I wanted to get students more involved with the material of the course. Second, I wanted to help a nonprofit organization that needed the help. Third, I wanted to develop student skills in writing for an audience other than a professor. Finally, I needed to rejuvenate the course for myself and make it more meaningful.

There is no question, that a project such as this involves students with the material of the course. Further, the very nature of this project is such that it involves them more than do other types of projects. When students selected their own nonprofit to study and did 6 assignments for that nonprofit, that was all the information they applied. In this project, although each student still only completes 6 individual application assignments, the class, as a whole, completes 46 assignments. The 46 assignments fall within 5 different categories. For example, one of those categories is labeled, "Developing a Customer Orientation," and consists of six assignments. Once I compile and edit the assignments within that category, I e-mail it to all the students who then, accidentally or on purpose, wade through all six assignment sections looking for their own section to edit. I see them paging through the developing document and they frequently make comments to me and to classmates about what they read there.

As for the second outcome, we certainly help nonprofits that need help – some desperately so. Like many nonprofits, the ARC chapter that we worked with had only a passing knowledge of marketing and how it could help their operations. Even in the for-profit sector, many people still equate marketing with advertising or personal selling and they tend to discount the need for marketing in their organization. One can easily understand why nonprofits, then, believe that marketing is something only big firms can afford and that if they only have a few dollars available for advertising they can make decisions themselves without the aid of marketing.

The Marketing Analysis that we provide, free-of-charge, contains sections on Developing a Customer Orientation, Strategic Planning and Organization, The Marketing Mix, Developing and Organizing Resources, and Planning and Controlling the Organization. Thus, the ARC chapter director was able to see that marketing is more than advertising or personal selling. Also, he is able to go directly to any section in which he is interested on any particular day or for any particular situation. Finally, rather than having to use a marketing textbook and apply the material himself, he has been able to read short explanations of concepts and read an application of the concept for his specific organization – already done. Where once I had to convince nonprofits to let me do an analysis for them, now I have a list of organizations (some for-profits!) that would like us to help them in the future.

As for the third objective – to develop student skills in writing for someone other than a professor – I believe that we are doing a disservice to students who write just for the teacher. As part of their assignment, students have to write for someone who, although intelligent and educated, may know little or nothing about marketing. So, terms that we take for granted in the discipline have to be defined. Concepts have to be explained. And this all has to be done diplomatically.

Further, at times in some analyses, we have to tell a nonprofit something unpleasant about itself. So, students learn how to tactfully explain an organization's faults and, perhaps more difficult, how to fix them. This is a skill that will be important in the real-world as students write up projects for their bosses and/or their clients. While honesty is the best policy, one has to learn how to be tactfully honest. This was an outcome that I had not considered at the beginning of the project but is now one that I expect.

Fourth, I instituted this project in order to rejuvenate the course and make it more meaningful for me. That objective was also reached. Lecture classes can get dull for the professor as well as the students. But, by developing this project I now have a sense that I'm more completely fulfilling my duties as a university professor. Not only do I believe that my teaching improved but I'm now more committed to service. The course is more than about explaining concepts, providing definitions, and giving examples. Now the concepts relate to the real world. Students and I get frustrated sometimes when we find constraints on what we can or may do in a nonprofit, but it is the same frustration felt by the managers of those nonprofits. I believe that what the students learn in this course is much more relevant to what they will be doing once they graduate. At the same time, I can still sneak in some of those concepts, definitions, and examples that are important.

Benefits and Challenges of The Project

The benefits of such a project as I have described are many, as are the challenges. For example, among challenges of the project is the amount of paperwork I have to look over, grade and re-grade. Indeed, sometimes it seems that I spend every spare minute handling the paperwork. But, in reality, I don't. The benefits of looking over assignments include making my job of grading them much, much easier. That's because the assignments are good. And, since many assignments are good, there is relatively little re-grading that has to be done. Although there are always a few students that are procrastinators and consistently do poor jobs on their assignments, most learn to do assignments earlier rather than later.

Another challenge is getting the very first assignment done. As I mentioned earlier, some students seem very fearful of completing assignments for which there is no 'correct answer' in an Instructor's Manual. However, once they complete the assignment and note that I give detailed feedback about what they missed and why I deleted points, they seem to gain confidence in their work. They also seem proud that they are contributing to a project that will actually be used by someone in the real world. With time, I have learned to be steadfast in my confidence in the students. And, time and time again, I find that they will rise to the challenge.

As a class we become very cohesive. Students see other students contributing good work to the document and this raises those students' reputations in the class. As a result of the increased level of cohesiveness, class discussions unrelated to the Marketing Analysis improve and are more fruitful for everyone.

Summary and Conclusions

When I started this type of project in my nonprofit marketing class, I was very hesitant and not at all sure that it was going to work. Now, however, I am looking for ways to introduce service learning into the other courses I sometimes teach – Sales Management, Principles of Marketing, Marketing Communications, and Consumer Behavior. The challenges are there but I believe are far outweighed by the benefits received by everyone involved. Not only do the students and the nonprofit benefit, but the university does as well. Potential faculty will likely more positively perceive a university or college that encourages its faculty to take risks in the classroom. Further, a university that encourages its faculty to reach out into the community and help where it can is likely to be more positively perceived by that community. The bottom line for the university is that outreach on the part of its faculty may lead to more donations and more tax-appropriated monies come budget time. Finally, individual faculty members benefit from service experiences as well. Not only do they build one's soul (as well as try it!), but I believe that service-oriented projects in the classroom may help faculty teach students that, in addition to being members of an academic community, we are also members of the larger communities in which we live.

Chapter Six

Organizational Communication

Steven J. Madden

Organizational Communication (SPCH 364) is required for all Communication, Marketing, and Business Management majors, which means that the student body in each class is interdisciplinary. It is my experience that students feel personally and academically enriched through their interaction with other majors. I find that this course is best taught, and has the largest pedagogical and applied effect, when I include real world outside assignments. With both considerations in mind, I combined two sections of SPCH 364 "Organizational Communication" to participate in service learning projects.

The normal structure for this course is one day each week I lecture on theory and share my personal experiences in business. On the remaining days, students do case analyses and Wall Street Journal presentations. While these activities engage students in practical applications, they never replace actual organizational contact. This is why I was so interested in the opportunity to develop this course incorporating a real-life experience as 40% of the content. The theories covered in the course include organizational theory, communication structure, group relationships, information technology, organizational culture, organizational diversity, power and conflict, communication networks, and strategic communication. These topics provide students with a greater understanding of how organizations communicate. What students do not experience is how these concepts and actions actually transpire through the daily activities of a company and its employees. To provide that applied pedagogical experience I developed a service learning project utilizing the Organizational Communication Evaluation Audit wherein students conduct an actual study (surveys, interviews, observations) of organizational communication theory and practices through partnering agreements with local organizations.

The benefits to the student were pedagogically sound. Students learned theory and also had an opportunity to relate this information to the very highest level of Bloom's Educational Taxonomy. I anticipated that the applied focus of this project would dramatically increase student awareness of the intricacies involved in multiple levels of organizational communication. Additionally, this type of experiential learning makes a significant contribution to higher education. According to Kolb, Lublin, Spoth, and Baker (1987) fieldwork [e.g. experiential/service learning] helps a student gain the competencies necessary to become an effective contributing member in the world of business. The learning objectives often demonstrated by students participating in an experiential project include:

> Behavioral Competence: Taking the initiative to seek information and propose a set of actions as a result of the search, all within the context of a certain organizational environment. Perceptual Competence: Identifying the correct problem(s), gathering, organizing, and interpreting information; and considering multiple perspectives. Affective Competence: Developing empathy and sensitivity to others' views, and managing discrepancies constructively. Symbolic Competence: Conceptualizing the business as a system of interrelated parts, considering how a change in one component affects the entire organization (p. 4).

Students experience real people, problems, results, and impacts which help to sharpen their professional skills (Buller, 1992) while achieving higher levels of self-confidence (Ramocki, 1987) and learning what it takes to function as responsible productive group [team] members Gundry & Buchko (1996).

Finally, I estimate that this type of assignment meets the criteria for service learning. It addresses community needs, is coordinated with an institution of learning, fosters civic responsibility, enhances academic curricula, and provides a structured time for students and participants to reflect on the service experience. Additionally, throughout the entire project students experienced the four elements of service learning which are as follows:

Preparation Phase:

Week one: Students were introduced, conceptually, to the service learning project through the acquisition and study of the "Pocket Guide to Service Learning," and through the guidance of the course professor. Weeks two & three: Students learned the process of identifying and reasoning those organization skills and variables initially associated with conducting an Organizational Communication Evaluation Audit. As the course progressed, students became more familiar with this process through theory lecture and personal experiences shared by the professor. Week three: Students divided into teams and participated in a Team Initiative Course, a low level ropes course that I have required in other classes with great success. During this period, students began planning their project around conducting an Organizational Communication Evaluation Audit. Week four: Students made initial contact with area business owners/managers to present their project idea and sought permission to conduct their project. In addition, under my direction, the students discussed any applicable letters/human subject questions. Week five: The teams scheduled site visits, gathered project material, and continued training on conduct and project application.

Action Phase:

Weeks six & seven: Since this project involved several nonprofit businesses with as many as 100 employees (supervisors and subordinates) some teams made additional company-wide presentations to explain the scope and purpose of their project, and to what extent they would interact with the organization's employees. Additionally, the students made it clear that participation was voluntary for everyone and assured complete confidentiality in all cases with project materials secured in the professor's office. Weeks eight & nine: The project continued with observations and surveys. Week ten: Teams analyzed data and observations. Week eleven, twelve & thirteen: Teams processed final project reports. Week fourteen: Teams presented their final projects.

Reflection Phase:

Observations: Throughout the various in-class and out-of-class activities the students learned how to critically observe the various elements that take place within dyadic, group, and meta-group communication networks of an organization. Journals: Students kept personal field journals to log their activities and comment on what they had done. This information included an analysis of what went right, wrong, or any new insights they gained about how people in organizations generally and specifically communicate in their daily activities of work. My focus at this point was to evaluate how the student put together facts, ideas, and experiences as a process of creating meaning.

Celebration Phase:

During a class dinner, each group member received a certificate of achievement signed by the Dean of the college, the top Administrator of the organization they worked with, and the course professor. The college and university newspaper also recognized their efforts through articles and feature stories.

The service component also benefited the community. Since organizations spend billions of dollars annually for training and development, it is clear that this type of organizational activity is mutually advantageous. For many smaller companies, it is often cost prohibitive to have this type analysis performed (5-25K). Additionally, smaller companies that expand rapidly have little experience or opportunity to explore such critical components as the efficiency or effectiveness of their current communication practices. Given that my institution is a land grant university it followed that a service learning project should provide services that are of value to the community which it serves.

Service Learning in the Class

Orientation & Training

For a project of this magnitude to be successful, it is critical that students fully understand their roles and responsibilities. Further, we must provide students with tools that allow them to conceptualize, understand, and execute their assignment. As I personally envisioned the course and project, I recognized at least three learning opportunities: (1) organizational communication (theory, concepts, and practices); (2) service learning (entering into a partnership with a community organization); and (3) experiential fieldwork (conducting research in an applied setting). To that end, I began the semester with an orientation in all three areas and allotted time in the remaining sessions for intensive training particular to each.

At the beginning of the semester a typical week included a ninety-minute theory/text lecture on Tuesdays followed by a Thursday class which was split into a forty-five-minute time slot for service learning and a forty-five-minute time slot for experiential fieldwork. Completing such a large project in one semester (approximately 15 weeks) demanded extreme focus during the first few weeks, which made the sessions quite intense. While this may seem a little aggressive, the rigorous schedule actually accomplished several important goals for both the students and me.

On day one, I explained in detail that we all had a unique opportunity this semester that required an enormous amount of energy, time, and dedication. I briefly discussed the objectives of the traditional course and then proceeded to incorporate material on service learning and experiential fieldwork. This led to a highly interactive dialogue about the particulars: the amount of out-of-class time required, how we would cover the actual class text in an accelerated fashion (the first six weeks), how we would incorporate an additional text on field casework (weeks 1-10) and a handbook on service learning (every week), what would be done in the project itself, the various potential personal, professional, and academic benefits, and a host of other topics. Frankly, I was excited about how much open discussion was happening on day one but I also understood that many students were using this time to decide whether or not to stay in the class.

On day two I lost 25 students between the two sections. While I anticipated some drop off, I was not expecting a 40% reduction. I began the second class discussing the project and requirements, and I felt optimistic about the level of commitment demonstrated by the remaining students. At that point, I knew the course would be a success because those who stayed WANTED the experience and were willing to make the extra effort required. As additional confirmation, the returning students had already purchased all the required books and had even read the first chapters in all three areas. From that day forward we all put 110% into each in-class and out-of-class activity. I should add that in subsequent semesters students have approached me weekly asking when, and if, I would be doing another Service Learning Project. Apparently, the word is out on how successful it was, despite the increased demands.

Service Learning Teams

The overall service learning project consisted of two upper-level undergraduate Organizational Communication classes, which I divided into four service learning teams (two teams per class). The hierarchical structure for the project went as follows: Project Administrator (course professor); Assistant Project Coordinators (four senior communication students who completed the Organizational Communication course in a previous semester); Project Managers (an individual student elected from each team); and finally Task Managers (various individuals from each of the four teams). Note that the percentage of majors represented in an average organizational communication course roughly breakouts as 30% Management, 30% Marketing, 10% Political Science, 20% Communication, and 10% other. Clearly, this is a multi-disciplinary class structure that typically results in a fascinating array of perspectives and approaches to course material.

Team Positions and Responsibilities

Obviously, the Project Administrator (i.e. the professor) has the ultimate project responsibility. This position establishes and provides project guidelines, general directions, coaching, mentoring, motivation, instruction, and conflict management interventions (if necessary). The notion of incorporating Assistant Project Coordinators was born out of a desire by several senior communication students to become involved in a hands-on practical application business project prior to graduation. Each of these students signed-up for an independent study (SPCH 499) and were charged with three responsibilities. Each student (1) identified and researched an area of interest in communication that correlated with the overall service learning project, (2) acted as a liaison between the Project Administrator and a service learning team, and (3) acted as a organizational communication project consultant for his respective team.

Following is an example of an Assistant Project Coordinator's independent study. One student was interested in researching the topic of "Emotional Intelligence." She started by conducting a literature review and then administered an "EI" pre-test on each member of the service learning team. Throughout the semester, she observed individual and team member interactions during class, at team meetings, and while on client site visits. At the end of the semester, she conducted an "EI" posttest, analyzed the quantitative and qualitative results, and produced a research paper that incorporated organizational communication, emotional intelligence, and service learning, along with her conclusions. Clearly, the benefits of acting as Assistant Project Coordinators were immeasurable. Each had an opportunity to conduct research, work in a leadership/consultant role, learn about organizational life in a real-time situation, and contribute to the experience of community citizenship. I took the liberty of expanding on the Assistant Project Coordinator because it is a creative way to handle large complex service learning projects in a productive and pedagogical manner where everyone wins.

Using several fieldwork guidelines established by Gundry & Buchko (1996), the following descriptions clarify the responsibilities of team and task leaders (i.e. Project Manager and Task Managers). Each Project Manager (PM) was responsible for being a team leader but not a boss! The duties included overseeing the entire project. They scheduled, coordinated, and performed administrative activities insuring the completion of individual and group assignments in an appropriate and timely manner. The PM also provided weekly project updates to the client, professor, and Assistant Project Coordinators. Additionally, the PM is responsible to team members. They maintained all files, delegated responsibilities in a balanced manner, served as the team's representative, and provided direction/information required by Task Managers. Their most important job is to facilitate effective communication between all concerned parties. Essentially, their job is to make sure that the Purpose of the project stays in the forefront of the teams' efforts. The role of the Project Manager is vitally important and one that should be discussed by the team, and assigned to someone who is committed to fulfilling the role. A bad PM results in a bad project and a bad deliverable. In the case of these four projects, team members elected the PM's from a group of individuals who indicated an interest in assuming the position.

Each service learning team also appointed several Task Managers (TM). The TM's were responsible for each of the major tasks within the framework of the project action plan and the project Time Management Schedule. Each major task on the project management chart had a Task Manager. Like the Project Manager, the team elected Task Managers according to their particular skills applicable to the task. The students looked for qualities such as open and effective communication abilities, strong interpersonal skills, motivation, dedication, and some sense of how to accomplish a particular task.

Note that during the formation of each service learning team I held concurrent class lectures on group development and group dynamics. Students learned about roles and norms. They also learned about group decision-making, group conflicts, motivation, and the importance of diverse perspectives. These turned out to be extremely important elements as projects advanced and different levels of individual time commitments and viewpoints surfaced.

Critical Thinking and Theory Application

A primary reason for engaging in this type of project is to extend and expand student opportunities for critical thinking and theory application. I determined that this project could fulfill these objectives and I incorporated Bloom's 1956 Taxonomy of Educational Objectives as one form of measurable outcomes. The six levels of Bloom's Taxonomy include: (1) To Know: Within the course on Organizational Communication the professor would be looking for the students' ability to remember and recognize information through in-class discussions; (2) To Comprehend: Exams throughout the course will test the students' ability to comprehend information that has been recalled; (3) To Apply: This is where the service learning project requires the students to apply the information presented in class to real organizational issues. This happens during the Action Phase when students are involved with conducting their project at organizational sites; (4) To Analyze: Again, during the Action Phase, I require students analyze the Organizational Communication Evaluation Audit they conducted with conscious knowledge of the parts and form of thinking; (5) To Synthesize: The creation of the final oral and written project presentation would identify the students' ability to synthesize material based on the information learned in class and experienced in the organization; (6) To Evaluate: This was achieved by:

A. The requirement of a personal field notebook during the entire project required the student to record events experienced in the field. I requested that these notes be self-reflective, include observations, and continually evaluate the various processes that took place. I also asked that they make judgments of right or wrong according to the standards presented in the course, by the participating organization, and foremost, those standards the students set for themselves.
B. Each team submitted a written account of its experiences in the field. This document included a description of fieldwork activities (e.g. observations, meetings, interviews, etc.); an assessment of present communication practices in the organization, including any communication training needs; and a summary/conclusion.

Service Learning Team Project

Overview

This course explores theories and practices of organizational communication from a critical, historical, and applied perspective. The primary objective of the course is to provide in-depth analytical treatments of issues analogous to the personal, relational, cultural, group, business, global, and ethical dimensions of everyday communication practices. A second objective is to apply course material to the organization and management of communication in professional contexts (i.e. Service Learning Project).

Description

Students enrolled in SPCH 364 conducted a semester long Organizational Communication Evaluation Audit (OCEA) of a company in the local region. The project involved site visits to participating companies, during which the teams focused on the current organizational communication practices in the company. To address this issue, student service learning teams interviewed corporate communicators and human resource personnel, observed communication practices in the host company, and conducted an organizational communication survey.

To help the companies meet their organizational communication objectives, the teams' field research sought to identify the strengths and limitations that support or inhibit effective communication and the potential skills and practices needed to overcome them. The companies that participated in the project were nonprofit organizations. I did not design this project specifically to work with this domain but after initial contacts were made with several organizations the first four to respond were nonprofits. These included a city police department, a city public works department, a university fire department, and a youth association for at risk juveniles.

Project Methodology

While in a larger sense one could argue that methodology is inherent in every aspect of the project, the term methodology, as it is used in this chapter, characterizes how students gathered information on the organizational communication practices in their respective client organizations rather than specific statistical or interpretive results born from analysis. While the teams referenced general results in their presentations, organization-specific data remained confidential. Each student service learning team conducted an Organizational Communication Evaluation Audit (OCEA). The OCEA incorporates several organizational communication variables, which are the theory/concepts in many organizational communication texts. While these theories/concepts are considered mainstream there are several communication scholars in particular whose work was primarily utilized: (1) Daniels and Spiker (1994) Organizational Communication Evaluation as a general perspective; (2) Dewine (1994) revised format of the ICA Communication Audit; and (3) Peterson & Pace (1976) Communication Climate Survey.

Designed to gather multiple sources of data, the OCEA creates a knowledge base which organizations can use to delineate conclusions about communication in specific instances. Daniels & Spiker (1994) state that this type of research serves the organizations' interests by (1) developing benchmarks so that management is aware of the status of the communication systems; (2) improving the internal communication system by identifying the factors which influence the system; (3) aids the management process of planning and control to allow better outcomes in the forms of employee satisfaction, adaptiveness, and performance; (4) improving the external communication system by providing information about environmental conditions affecting the organization; and (5) bridging existing organizational communication gaps.

Procurement of data occurs in a multitude of ways. One is the use of direct observation of the organization's communication activities by the researcher. The second method is the interview. Interviews allow the researcher to gather specific as well as general information from individuals and/or groups within the organization. The third method is the survey questionnaire that can range from highly structured to open-ended questions designed to measure attitude, communication climate, supportiveness, satisfaction, etc.

While service learning teams obtained organizational communication data using each of these methods, the communication components found in the survey questionnaire provided a "desired information" structure. In other words, those areas outlined in the survey where also those communication variables investigated in other data gathering activities. The two-part survey included several communication variables. Part One of the survey included statements requiring a response on employee perceptions of how much or how little they (1) received information from others; (2) sent information to others; (3) received a follow-up on information that is sent; (4) engaged in communication relationships; and (5) were satisfied with the communication within the organization. Part Two of the survey included statements requiring a Likert scale response on trust, participatory decision making, supportiveness, openness to downward communication, and concerns for high performance goals.

Additionally, students looked for other communication activities they thought interesting or applicable to
the project assignment.

Each service learning team had two choices in terms of statistical analysis. The first option was to report data in terms of percentages (e.g. 25% agreed, 10% disagreed, etc.). I felt this option had to be included for several reasons: (1) if a team worked on a project where the organization had a large employee base the time to conduct higher level statistical procedures on a large data set might have been prohibitive; (2) many organizations prefer information reported in terms that are less complex (e.g. discrepancies reported in percentages may be easier to understand than p values or levels of significance; and (3) if a particular team felt uncomfortable with more advanced statistics I wanted them to know they had an option. The second option was to enter survey results into a data file and analyze the data via SPSS including frequencies, cross-tabulations, and correlation. Of the four teams, three opted for the percentage option and one chose the SPSS option.

Meetings

Each team met with members of the host company several times during the semester. The first visit was to sign an agreement with the company including what the team would provide in terms of deliverables (analysis, research, and recommendations); a time table for the project; protocol for visits; and protocol for conducting on-site research. The second visit consisted of a tour of the company, during which time the team obtained general information about the structure of the organization, communication issues, practices, and other related details. The third visit focused on interviews and/or observations. The fourth visit involved conducting a survey with all or a significant sample of the organization's employees. The final meeting took place at the host site or at the course classroom. At that time, the team made a final research presentation of their analysis as well as a short discussion period to answer any further questions the host company had. Additionally, each team met approximately fifteen times out-of-class for the purpose of planning, progress reports, adjustments to the plan, statistical analysis, and preparation of the final written document and public presentation.

Managing the Project

These four service learning projects followed a process model developed by Gundry and Buchko (1996). The model includes an Assessment Phase, Implementation Phase, and a Result Phase. Note that before any contract was signed to perform a project with a client each team essentially worked through and developed an initial prospectus covering the elements from all three phases. While this may initially seem as though I was "putting the horse before the cart," there were several important reasons why I did this: (1) the size of the project was fairly large and complex and therefore, it was important that each of the elements be thought-out and understood; (2) time was an extremely important variable. The course lasted 15 weeks. In that time students attended weekly lectures, studied a textbook on organizational communication, took exams, wrote essays, and conducted their service learning project (average project time per student was approximately 45 hours). Time was critical, and I did not want to commit to my students or a company this experience if I did not feel could be reasonably fulfilled; (3) since these were undergraduate students I also felt an obligation to provide a substantial amount of guidance, coaching and mentoring throughout the process; (4) students deserved an opportunity to decide the cost/benefit ratio of such a large commitment in relation to their other studies and personal goals before the drop/add deadline. With that in mind, the following outline depicts the stages of project development, implementation, and completion.

Assessment Phase

Information Gathering & Preliminary Analysis

Given the time constraints of a semester I took it upon myself to initiate contact with potential clients before accepting the project. From previous professional engagements, I had some notion of which companies in the surrounding area might be open to such discussions and subsequently made the appropriate inquiries. This effort resulted in the acquisition of four companies who stated a strong interest in the project and the potential deliverables.

Each company provided me with general information such as mission statements, company structure, products, and so on which I then passed on to the student team who would be conducting the project for that company. This provided each team with a basic understanding of each company and a starting point for further research such as a broader scope of the particular industry, its operating environment, and any particular political-economic-social-technological concerns.

Establishing the Purpose & Scope of the Project

Within the Project Purpose three questions must be answered: First it must be determined what the team intends to do and why. Second, it must be determined how the team intends to do the project. The third and final question is what does the team intend to provide the client. Essentially this information gives an overall structure to the project experience. In the projects, the purpose and scope was determined primarily by the course professor, but it was important that all student team members and the client clearly understood these components because ultimately they became the "Deliverable." In the case of the Organizational Communication Course, the deliverable takes on a dual identity. The deliverable is a major part of the course grade for each team. Perhaps more important, the deliverable is the product or service that the student team creates for a real client, the results
of which may have an affect on company employees whom the students, in many instances, have never met. The importance of the deliverables is real and carries a high level of responsibility for the students, professor, and client.

Initial Meeting with Client

Once each team has gathered and discussed information from secondary sources about the company and the project purpose and scope, the client was called to arrange for the first face-to-face meeting. This is a fairly anxious and exciting time for both parties. Clearly, for most students, this is the first time they have had an opportunity to meet the top administrator of a company plus they are also there to negotiate and sign a contract for services. Yes, this was a nervous time. It was also a time that gave the students an opportunity to experience a real-world business engagement and understand a higher level of commitment, a commitment to a real company and to the lives of real people vs. a hypothetical textbook simulation.

Here are some student comments about their initial client meeting:

I was very nervous thinking about meeting the president of a company but he turned out to be a very friendly and caring person."
I was sure that we were going to be laughed at . . . I mean here we are a bunch of undergraduate students asking someone to let us come in and evaluate how their company communicates . . . I was amazed at the reception. . . they actually wanted us to be there . . . it was like we were doing them a big favor . . . it made me realize that we had something to offer.

At first we were all somewhat intimidated by the building, the offices, and the people but once we did our introductions and the people all smiled at us I was sure this was going to work out just fine -- as long as we were professional and produced quality work.

For the first time since entering college I felt like a professional . . . I am confident that my future holds many exciting experiences.

The Contract

The contract, for this project, is an extremely important document. The purpose of the agreement is to clarify and commit to conditions that will govern the project, and the relationship between the service learning project team and the principal parties of the company with whom they will work. I designed the structure for the contract and then left the negotiations for meetings and any other associated services up to the students and the client. Each contract included (1) Service Learning Team Goals (these are based on the definition of service learning - Duckenfield and Wright, 1997; (2) Purpose of the Project (what the students will be doing for the client organization); (3) How To Accomplish Project Objectives (this is the time line for meetings and activities to perform the project); (4) Team Members & Positions (this is a list of all the team members including a contact phone number and their responsibilities within the team); (5) Final Comments (a final note of appreciation and statement of team commitment to the project); and (6) Contract Signatures (in triplicate - one for the client, one for the team, and one for the professor). See appendix for sample contract.

Implementation Phase

A successful service learning project requires clearly defining the client's expectations, agreeing on the purpose and scope of the project, providing clear communication to all members of the team, and carefully managing the plan. Since these projects had several levels of administration and various layers of interaction, it was extremely critical to develop specific objectives for the project.

Objectives must be clearly defined, measurable, attached to time frames, and attainable in order to complete the project purpose. To achieve the numerous objectives associated with this service learning project each team had to assign various individuals and sub-groups to specific components of the project. Essentially, the objectives identify what the team must do. The objectives for each of the four projects included the following:

1. Preliminary Analysis
2. Industry Analysis
3. Establish Project Purpose
4. Client Meeting #1 (Contract)
5. Client Meeting #2 (Company Tour & Observations)
6. Client Meeting #3 (Observations & Interviews)
7. Client Meeting #4 (Organizational Communication Evaluation Surveys)
8. Analysis (Analyze OCE surveys - quantitative/qualitative)
9. Write Final Report
10. Final Client Meeting (Provide client with Final Written Report & Presentation)

To determine how the teams could accomplished their objectives they had to develop an action plan.

Action Plan

The action plan specifically identifies what activities and steps the team and each of its members must perform to satisfy the stated objectives. Each team took their objectives and created a Project Management Time Chart that corresponded with the fifteen-week semester schedule (See example in appendix). Although the time chart required adjustment throughout the entire project, it was an essential element in successfully meeting personal, educational, and professional goals for all of the teams in the two classes. The Objectives of the project make up the action plan. Task Managers charted each objective along a time-line on the Project Management Chart. This gave each team a visual graphic representation of what it had to do, who was in charge of a specific objective (Task Managers), how much time each Task Group had to perform its assignment, and where the overall service learning team and individual task groups were in relation to project plan and deadlines (see following partial example).

[Action Plan / Project Management Chart]

Weeks: 1 2 3 4 5 6 7 8 9 10 11 12 13 14 15
Objectives:

1. Preliminary Analysis   X X
2. Industry Analysis   X X X X
3. Establish Project Purpose X X
4. Client Meeting #1   X
5. Client Meeting #2   X
6. Client Meeting #3   X
7. Client Meeting #4   X
8. Analysis   X X X X
9. Write Final Report   X X
10. Final Client Meeting   X

Each week the project manager and each of the individual task managers gave a presentation to the class, reporting their progress on activities within the project action plan and the overall status of the project. These weekly presentations accomplished several things: (1) teams and individual team members got to hear differing perspectives on what was done and the level of success in how the other team approached various tasks; (2) students learned about the other team's client organization; and (3) members from each team could share experiences and brainstorm possible alternatives for accomplishing future activities.

Results Phase / Deliverable(s)

Written Organizational Report

Each team presented its client/organization with a fifty (50) page Organizational Communication Evaluation Audit report which included the following: (1) an executive summary discussing the scope and purpose of the project and brief outline of their findings; (2) a description of their Organizational Communication Evaluation Audit survey and its purpose; (3) a preliminary analysis of the client's organization (e.g. mission statements, products, size. etc.) and a general industry analysis; (4) a section on the group's impression of the organization including the initial meeting, the tour, observational meetings, and the survey visit; (5) a data analysis section discussing the methodology utilized and subsequent statistical interpretations including graphs; (6) a conclusion section covering the team's interpretation of the results, suggestions on how to address some of the areas where improvement could be made, and any limitations of the study; (7) and an appendix that included a copy of the contract, a sample survey, tabulation results, graphs, organizational charts, and references.

The Organizational Report was Priority Mailed to the client approximately one week before the oral multimedia presentation so that the client would have time to read the report and ask any questions of the team.

Oral/Multi-media Organizational Report

Each team provided a brief synopsis of its written report, with time for questions from other class members, the host client, and me. Topics covered included: (1) the relationship of fieldwork (service learning) to an education in organizational communication and interaction with the community; (2) the communication strengths and weaknesses found in the client organization; (3) how well the team functioned in the field; (4) the best/worst examples of the field experience; and (5) recommendations for future work by next years' students. Each team had 45 minutes to deliver their presentation. I required a presentation consistent with professional public speaking guidelines including professional dress, minimal use of note cards or key word outlines, creative use of multimedia(s), loud-clear voices, eye contact, correct grammar, appropriate supporting materials, etc.

Evaluations

Individual

➤ **Class Participation:** Involvement during class was required and expected.

➤ **On-site Attendance:** To conduct a team project at a client's organization team members must be there! I took attendance at each scheduled site visit and team members had to participate for the entire scheduled time.

➤ **Project Journals:** Each student kept a personal field journal about what went right, what went wrong, and any insights gained in terms of how people communicated in their daily activities within their organizations, in general and specifically. I was looking for how each student put together facts, ideas, and experiences as a process of creating meaning based on what they read in the course text and experienced in the field. I required the journal be typed or word processed, free of spelling and grammatical errors, that each entry be dated, and be approximately 10 pages long.

➤ **Personal Experience Essays:** These two essays provide each student with an opportunity to articulate ~in writing~ how the material they were reading applied to their experiences with team members and with the client. Each student had to construct a 3 to 5 typed and double spaced page story, ~complete with dialogue and drama~ of a scene from their organizational experiences. At the end of the essay, I required a two or three paragraph theoretical explanation of what their illustration demonstrated, using and referencing the dialogue as primary data.

➤ **Quizzes:** Since the temptation to fall behind in reading and mastery of course material has a disastrous effect on student performance I gave two quizzes covering reading and lecture material on a regular schedule. These quizzes had approximately 40 questions and focused on theories, research findings, and applications. We graded each quiz in class and the team with the highest cumulative score on the two quizzes, plus the two personal experience essays, added 5 points to their final exam score.

> **Final Exam:** This was a comprehensive examination covering all course materials with the emphasis on reading. At this point in the semester, I expected students to have a thorough understanding of course material and an ability to reflect their education and experiences in a clear concise manner. The exam included approximately 100 questions.

Team

> **Team Initiative Training:** I required team members to participate in a Team Initiative Course at the Clemson Outdoor Laboratory. This activity kicked-off their service learning team project.

> **Team Evaluations:** Team members completed individual teamwork assessments that I provided to account for the work of the team, the team members, and the person doing the evaluation. The students submitted these evaluations toward the end of the semester.

> **Client Site Activity Evaluation:** Members of the client organization evaluated the student team in terms professionalism, meeting contract agreement, interaction while on-site, communication on and off site, and other agreed upon elements.

> **Final Organizational Report:** Each team submitted a written account of its experiences in the field, which included (1) an introduction and literature review; (2) description of fieldwork activities (e.g. interviews, observations, surveys, etc.); (3) an assessment of present communication activities and practices (e.g. analysis of interviews, observations, and surveys); (4) a summary, conclusion, and recommendations. The written report could not exceed 50 double spaced pages including charts, graphs, and references. Papers were typed or word processed, free of spelling and grammatical errors, and demonstrated creative intelligence.

> **Final Oral/Multi-media Research Presentation (15%):** Each team delivered a brief synopsis of its written report, leaving time for questions from class members, the host client, and me. Topics included: (1) the relationship of fieldwork (service

learning) to an education in organizational communication and interaction with the community; (2) the communication strengths and weaknesses found in the client organization; (3) how well the team functioned in the field; (4) the best/worst examples of the field experience; and (5) recommendations for future work by next year's students. Each team had approximately 45 minutes for this report. Presentations were consistent with professional public speaking guidelines, including professional dress, minimal use of note cards or key word outlines, creative use of multimedia, loud-clear voices, eye contact, correct grammar, appropriate supporting materials, etc.

Benefits and Challenges of Service Learning

Throughout this paper, I have outlined the numerous benefits and challenges of conducting a service learning project. I could write an entire book in this area alone, so as I conclude this piece, I endeavor to share a few more examples of the enriching experience that service learning affords those fortunate enough to participate.

Students

For the students the benefits of service learning are everlasting, but I also consider these experiences an integral part of the maturation process. Clearly, the students in these projects experienced personal growth. They displayed increased self-confidence as well as a sense of identity and self-respect. Social growth was also evident in terms of interpersonal and communication skills. Intellectual growth was present throughout the entire process. Students not only advanced in cognitive and critical thinking skills, but they also developed a desire to learn new ideas and concepts. Perhaps the most rewarding experience for me was observing their newfound obligation to citizenship. Each student reported a sense of contributing to the community and an awareness of community needs. They truly felt as though they were giving back to society. They were very proud of their involvement.

The old adage goes "there is no gain without pain" and these students experienced their share of pain. Their first big hurdle was time. Each student knew from the start that he or she would be spending more time in this class than others. In fact, by week four, one student established that "...we spend more time on this class than a combination of all our other classes." While this was a major time management adjustment, they all ultimately persevered. Each team experienced conflict. Conflicts extended from personal to group to professional. One person not doing his or her share, team meetings, schedules, employees at the client organization not always being helpful, and countless others. As I hoped, part of their experiential learning was to navigate and survive in real-time and real-life situations. They committed to a project and willingly accepted the responsibility, which ˜in the end˜ allowed them to handle setbacks. Consequently, they experienced growth both personally and professionally.

Professor

For me the benefits were renewed sense of vigor, excitement, and enthusiasm about teaching. Few times in my life have I seen students accept so much responsibility and produce a project that demonstrated such a high level of professionalism. The more they got excited, the more I got excited. The more they wanted to experiment and experience, the more I wanted to guide them. This experience was, in its purest form, a win-win situation for all of us. No, it was not easy, but it was worthwhile and important. At times, I felt my life revolved around grading reports, papers, and tests, and attending meetings. I lived and breathed these projects. As I witnessed the high level of academic, personal, and professional growth taking place I knew that I, too, was being moved in ways that I did not want to lose. I needed this remarkable experience as much as my students did. We were fully engaged in this journey.

University

The university gained considerably from these projects. In a fashion, they were meeting their mission of public service, and ˜in the process˜ gained new partners in the community. Our students, as ambassadors of Clemson University, overcame many barriers that often exist between academia and the public. The ultimate benefit to the university is having professors who accept the challenge of developing exciting, innovative, and academically effective courses to prepare students for successful careers.

Community

The final beneficiary is the community. Collaboration between higher education and the community build a strong sense of society for all involved. When we combine innovation with education, the rewards are far reaching. All four clients involved in this project reported how valuable the final reports were to their organization. More importantly was how appreciative they were to have an opportunity to interact with mature, professional, and enthusiastic young people. The employees of these companies enjoyed working with the students and were genuinely interested in the results of the project. Supervisors noted that during this project morale was noticeably higher in the organization.

Summary and Conclusion

Clearly, service learning provides one avenue for the development of educational and community partnerships resulting in a potential strengthening of society. Courses such as the one outlined in this chapter become a salient means through which students and professors support a nurturing environment for learning and progress. The mission of becoming responsible citizens ~preparing for careers and respecting diversity of opinions~ is a goal one can hardly resist. Griggs & Stewart (1997) pull the whole notion of service learning together by stating "[t]he lesson in community building lies in the fact that the sum of the parts is stronger than any single component" (p. 187). Every time we work together, we contribute one more small part to the greater good of humanity.

Works Cited

Brown, S & Duckenfield, M (1997). Service learning pocket guide. National Dropout Prevention Center, Clemson University, Clemson, S.C.

Buller, P. F. (1992). Reconceptualizing the small business consulting course: A response to the Porter and McKibbin criticisms. *Journal of Management Education, 16 (1).* 56-75.

Daniels, T. D. & Spiker, B. K. (1994). *Perspectives on organizational communication* (3rd eds.). Brown & Benchmark, Dubuque, IA.

Daniels, T. D., Spiker, B. K. & Papa, M. J. (1997). *Perspectives on organizational communication* (4th ed.).

DeWine, S. (1994). *The consultants craft: Improving organizational communication.* St. Martin,s Press, New York, NY.

Griggs, H. & Stewart, B. (1997). Community building in higher education: To bring diverse groups together with common goals. *Education, 117, (2),* p.183.

Gundry, L. K. & Buchko, A. A. (1996). *Field casework: Methods for consulting to small and startup businesses.* SAGE, Thousand Oaks, CA.

Kolb, D., Lublin, S., Spoth, J., & and Baker, R. (1987). Strategic management development: Using experiential learning to assess and develop managerial competencies. *Journal of Management Development, 5,* 13-24.

Madden, S. J. (1998). *Organizational communication workbook.* Clemson University, Clemson, SC.

Peterson, B. D. & Pace, R .W. (1983). Communication climate and organizational satisfaction. In Pace, R. W. & Faules, D. F. (eds.), *Organizational communication.* Prentice Hall, Englewood Cliffs, New Jersey.

Ramocki, S. (1987). Measured effectiveness of client-sponsored projects in the marketing research course. *Journal of Marketing Education, 9,* 24-30.

Sample Contract

Service Learning Project Agreement

The purpose of this agreement is to clarify and commit to conditions that will govern the project relationship between the Service Learning Project team (Organizational Communication SPCH 364 / Clemson University) and the principal parties of _____.

Service Learning Team Goals

The primary goal of our Service Learning Team is to conduct a service learning project where student team members learn and develop through active participation in thoughtfully organized service that:

- Is conducted to meet the needs of a community organization.
- Is coordinated with an institution of higher education.
- Helps foster civic responsibility.
- Is integrated into and enhances the academic education of the student.
- Provides time for participants to reflect on the service experience.

Purpose of Project

The purpose is to provide (client) with a communication evaluation of his organization. This evaluation includes but is not limited to examining types of information/communication, amounts of information/communication, communication relationships, and overall communication climate.

How to Accomplish These Objectives

The Service Learning Team will need to conduct at least five (5) team/client meetings:

1. *Sign Project Agreement:*
   During this meeting team members and the client discussed the project, asked each other questions, established the parameters for a working relationship, discussed time and personnel requirements, and decided on whether or not to sign the agreement.
2. *Tour of Organization:*
   During this visit team members will tour the organization with the intent of learning more about, company structure, employees, products, communication, and other elements of daily organizational activity.

3. *Communication Observation:*
    During this visit the team will be broken down into smaller groups and
    request an opportunity to visit, for example, different departments and
    areas of the organization with the intent of observing how people
    communicate in the activities of their jobs.

4. *Conduct Organizational Communication Survey:*
    During this visit, the team will provide all organizational members with
    a copy of a survey to be filled out within 30 minutes and collected at
    the end of that time. Prior to the last meeting the client will be sent a
    final organizational communication evaluation report for the company.
    This is done so that the client can ask additional questions at the final
    presentation and have a greater understanding of the project analysis.

5. *Multi-media Oral Presentation:*
    At this time, the client will come to the Organizational Communication
    SPCH 364 class for a team presentation of the entire Service Learning
    Project.

Team Members & Project Positions

Name, major, position, contact numbers.

Final Comments

We appreciate the opportunity your organization is providing us. We will
approach this project with the highest level of professionalism and
consideration. Your organization will be informed on a weekly basis as to our
progress and any other items that you would like to discuss. Thank you for your
cooperation and we encourage you to ask any questions or provide us with any
comments during this project. We are looking forward to working with you
and your company.

Chapter Seven

Business Writing

Elizabeth C. Rice

Abstract

We read and hear that college students need to be "more employable." That upon graduation, they must be able to team with others, use computer spreadsheets and databases, analyze and interpret data and on and on. So, how do we incorporate these skills of the workplace into our college curricula? In the past, I assigned believable, yet imaginary, recipients for the assigned memos, letters, and reports for my business and technical writing students. Now my students take "issues" from their community and work toward solutions in interdisciplinary teams. After generating a proposal for their project, the students create a "deliverable" for their client and present their project in a multimedia trade show presentation to their peers, faculty and college administration, and their client. Their memos and letters are sent to real people, the interviews, surveys, and graphs represent real information, and each project addresses a real need or issue in the community.

Incorporate Service Learning in Technical and Business Writing Classes

I teach two sections of Business Writing or Technical Writing each semester, and I know that students learn better when they are actively learning. I incorporate service learning into my curricula because students tell me it works. An agricultural engineer said, "For me, the service learning project brought about a real sense of accomplishment. The fund-raiser was something I worked hard at and I could see my work unfold and know that I had accomplished something." A graphic design student said, "The community project was a big part of the semester for me. It is where I learned the most about myself. I felt a sense of belonging in the class with them. I also felt like I really contributed a useful piece of information for Clemson students on date rape with the publication of our brochure."

In business and technical writing classes, students learn how to write memos, letters, proposals, and reports. They also need to learn how to use and incorporate multimedia into presentations, how to work collaboratively and successfully on interdisciplinary teams, and how to communicate effectively in a professional manner in today's workplace using electronic mail. Over the course of the service learning projects, each student learns by actively using these skills. Each student writes a memo that outlines what service learning project they plan to work on, and then they form interdisciplinary teams after determining each team member's strengths and skills. They then collaboratively write a proposal based on a proposal criteria sheet given to them when we discuss the projects. Throughout the project, the students send weekly e-mail progress reports to me and communicate weekly via e-mail, phone, or in person with their client. Finally, the team creates a multimedia presentation complete with a published "deliverable" for a trade show conference held at a nearby professional conference center.

Introducing Service Learning to Students

On the second day of class, I explain that a requirement of the class (worth 30% of their total grade) is to work on an interdisciplinary team to create a service learning project and produce a "deliverable." For many students, doing a community or volunteer project is not a new idea; what is new is that they will be doing something they care about and get credit and a grade for it. Many of them have wonderful ideas of ways they can help their community. In the past, I assigned students to projects, but I have learned the hard way that it is always best when students pick their own project. From the start they have a sense of "ownership" and they are more actively engaged and involved in the project. One architecture student said, "I liked the way you helped us get the project going, and then you got out of the way."

I "help" the students choose projects in two different ways. One way is that I ask them to number from one to ten. I then ask them to brainstorm in the following manner:

- One and two are things/issues that affect them personally;
- three and four are things/issues that affect their age team or college students in general;
- five and six are things that affect their community/town/state (this community may be their college community or their home community);
- seven and eight are national issues/racial issues/gender issues/socioeconomic or age issues;
- nine and ten are global issues.

Each student brainstorms on paper to try to create a solution (and thus a project) for one or all of the problems or issues they articulated. This can be done individually or in small teams. Their lists and their solutions always pleasantly surprise me. This is when once again my faith is renewed in the younger generation. They do care, and they want to find solutions to some of the issues and problems that plague all of us as a society.

My colleague, Barbara Weaver, does it a little differently. She asks her students to think of people, organizations, or businesses that need help and she goes from there. Both ways work and we find that offering two different approaches to finding a partner allows the students to explore a variety of issues/ideas.

How Teams are Selected for the Service Learning Projects

When I first started doing service learning projects in the classroom, I allowed students to get into teams on their own. There was no criteria or selection process; often the students would pair up or get into teams with students they knew from other classes or with whomever sat closest to them. Since then I have learned the importance of team selection based on skills and abilities in addition to the specific service learning topic or issue. Using the "Skills of Life" (see Figure 1) each student circles three to four skills that they are proficient in and two skills that they are weak in. By focusing on skills first, I am encouraging the students to begin to envision themselves as team members who have specific skills and abilities to contribute to their team.

Since I have begun to incorporate the skills assessment method, the discussion in class on the day that teams are being formed is centered on what skills and abilities each student has to offer a specific team. Once they form the teams, I ask them to discuss both the strengths and weaknesses of the team members – this way they can really begin to see the team dynamics and begin to watch for where the team will succeed and where potential pitfalls may be. I also ask each team to determine the roles best suited for each team member – who is best at time management or computer skills, etc. From the start of their service learning projects, the students are more aware and "tuned into" each individual's strengths and weaknesses and the skills needed for a successful team and project completion.

Time Allowed for Service Learning Projects

On the average, I introduce the service learning project on the second day of class, but it isn't until the third week of class that the teams really get down to work. I teach on Tuesdays and Thursdays and usually allow five to six weeks for the SL project. Once the project is under way, Tuesdays are set aside for a half class period of status reports and Thursdays are workdays for the teams.   Occasionally, the class determines that we do not need to meet every Tuesday for status updates.

Many faculty require team projects but don't allow class time for the students to work. If I value the work, which I do, then I need to allow class time for the students to work. Many of our clients work from 8:30-4:30 Monday through Friday, not Sunday evening from 6-9 in the library, which is when and where the majority of student team work often takes place. The students need the time during the working day to contact their clients, get to the print shop, and to meet each other.

Student Service Learning Projects

Because I allow the students to choose their own service learning projects (with my final approval), I usually have 8-12 projects per semester. Although this sometimes makes for some chaos, confusion, and more work for me to grade, it also means more opportunities for service, more brochures and booklets – more for the community. Last spring, the students undertook the following projects:

Save a Life: Learn Health and Safety at the Red Cross

One of the students, a Health Science major, recently had a friend's father suffer from a heart attack. He had enrolled in a Red Cross CPR class at home soon after and he wanted to see more college students get involved and get trained. After conducting a survey, the team of three was surprised to find out how few college students knew CPR and how few knew about the Pickens County Red Cross programs. There was a real need to inform the students about the local Red Cross chapter and of the courses available. The student team created a brochure for the Pickens County Red Cross aimed primarily at local college students that highlighted the classes offered locally. The brochure was "delivered" to the client and the students published their work by printing the brochure and distributing it in the dorms and at the student health center.

Donate Your Brain: Join the Calhoun Society

Two of the team members are members of the Calhoun Society, an honor society on campus. After conducting a survey, which they created and distributed, the team discovered that only a few students were aware of the Calhoun Society and its purpose. The student team created a public relations packet which highlights the Calhoun Society's purpose, admission requirements, etc., so Clemson University students can be better informed about the honor society and its function on campus. After the trade show, several other students in the class joined the Calhoun Society; they admitted that before the presentation they had either never heard of the Society or they did not know the criteria for admission.

Make an Executive Decision: Join the Chamber of Commerce

The father of one student is a member of the local Chamber of Commerce and had recently expressed the need for a brochure to promote membership in the local Chamber. The students worked with the Chamber to develop and publish the brochure. The night of the presentations, many of the Chamber of Commerce members came to see the presentation and brochure.

I Can't Get Breast Cancer: I'm only in College: What College Women Need to Know About Breast Cancer

A secondary education major's mother had recently been diagnosed with breast cancer. The student's mother convinced her daughter of the need to alert college women to the risks of breast cancer and the benefits of monthly self-examinations.   Working with the campus health center, the nursing department, and information from the Internet, this team of four created a brochure for college women. At the tradeshow, the team handed out pink ribbons and their brochure. The team said that many of the college women who stopped at their table really thought that breast cancer was something that only their mothers and grandmothers needed to think about.   One interesting note about this project is that one of the team members, a male education student, said that he gave the brochure to his girlfriend and mother and explained to them what he had learned from working on this project. He said that at first he didn't feel like the project had anything to do with him, but after completing the brochure and learning about breast cancer, he said that he was part of a community and responsible to it. He also learned that men can get breast cancer as well.

Why Do I Feel This Way? Depression

A computer science major had been diagnosed with depression and helped by the college health center. She wanted to let others know that there was help close by. Working with the counselors at the health center, the three-person team developed a brochure on depression and a web site for the counseling center.

Copyrighting, Cooper, and Clemson University

This three-person team "signed up" for this project. I had been approached earlier by a reference librarian who was concerned that college students didn't know the laws about copyright. She suggested that a team of students create a brochure and that the library would publish it and have it available at the reference desk for students. Many of the students were amazed to find out the "real" story behind copyrighting.

Trees? Now You Know: Botanical Garden Tree Identification Guide

Two forestry students and one computer science student teamed up and created a brochure for children on tree identification. They selected ten trees native to our region and scanned the actual leaves to create their booklet. Each leaf is life-size and the actual color of the leaf is correctly produced. These spiral bound booklets are available at the South Carolina Botanical Garden for visitors to pick up. As they walk along, visitors, especially children, can use the booklet to help identify trees native to South Carolina found in the Botanical Garden and learn the various uses of these trees.

Give a Hand to Helping Hands

Helping Hands is the local thrift storefront that raises money to help battered and abused women and children in our area. College students always have lots of extra "stuff" and when Christmas and summer rolls around, they often throw out unwanted clothing and furniture in the nearest dumpster instead of putting these to good use by recycling them. This team consisted of three students, who had plenty of prior experience in helping others in their communities, although, curiously enough, not one of them had heard of Helping Hands since they had been at college. They decided that students needed to be made aware of the opportunities to help in their college community. The brochure they created explained to students what Helping Hands is, where they could drop off things, and ways they could get involved if they had the time.

FREE FOOD (Nutrition for the College Student)

A nursing student and two team members wanted to make college students more aware of fat and nutrition. They originally decided to create a brochure for the students, but then one of them came up with the idea of a doorknob hanger. Each resident advisor could hang this "brochure" on dormitory doors or apartment doors at the beginning of the school year. The "doorknob hanger" explains the new nutritional triangle and what good nutrition is. The students also give examples of fat content in the foods that many college students eat – fast foods. The brochure offers examples of alternative meals that are low in fat and explains the importance of exercise, drinking fluids, and getting plenty of rest.

Mirror, Mirror on the Wall, Who's the Fattest One of All? (Common Eating Disorders)

Three female students teamed up to fight against eating disorders. Two of the women have close friends with eating disorders and felt that many college women are in grave danger. Working with the college health center and reliable Internet sites, the team created a brochure that outlines the danger signs and shows where help is available. The team was both amazed and horrified when other female students began talking about their own or friend's experiences with eating disorders. After completing this project, the team felt that currently not enough attention is being paid to eating disorders on campuses or in the media. They were concerned that many young women are not really aware of the dangers associated with eating disorders and how to get help. They thought that a good extension of the project would be for college women to go out into middle and high school classes to discuss eating disorders.

What Happened to Me Last Night? (Dangers of Rohypnol, GHB, and Ketamine)

Three other women teamed up to fight back against a growing concern and danger – the increase of date rape drugs on college campuses. Several months before, three local college students had been arrested with these drugs and charged with intent to distribute. These women felt that there wasn't enough information "out there" for college women to be educated and alerted to these very dangerous drugs. Using radio spots, testimonials from women who had been date-raped and current information, they created this informative brochure. The college health center was overjoyed to have a current brochure to distribute. They also sent it to the local rape crisis center and the local police and sheriff departments. One of the team members who is very shy said that she was very happy to know that she could make a real difference. She said that, "if she can save one women from being date-raped," she felt that her project was very successful and a wonderful service to her community. All three women said that, by just doing the project, they had learned much about date rape and date rape drugs.

These projects satisfy my requirements of the class, but more importantly, they answer the need(s) of the individual team members. Most of the projects mirror the fears, hopes, and concerns of my students.

How to Monitor Multiple Projects

Using progress reports, both written via e-mail and oral in class, I can keep a fairly close eye on the projects. One thing I have come to believe since doing service learning is that it is important for the students to *really* control the project and its progress and outcomes. They must be allowed to sink or swim. We learn from our failures, but in the traditional classroom, we rarely allow our students to learn this valuable lesson. Using weekly e-mail progress reports from the teams helps me see how things are going. They must report what they accomplished, what they plan to do, and as one student put it, the "speed bumps" they have encountered. The students report to me and can ask for help anytime along the way.

I find that I listen attentively to the tone of the report and for what is not written. In the report, they must include the individual team members' accomplishments over the week, so I can clearly see who is working and showing up for the meetings and who is not. In addition, each team must report orally to the class once a week. This ensures that I see all of the students and that they get help from their peers as well as from me. The day of the status reports is exciting; the teams are usually eager to share their project and progress with the class. Last spring, one team was having quite a few problems and voiced their disappointment in dealing with "real" clients. Many other teams shared their frustrations. The next week, the rest of the class was eager to see how well things were going for the team.

How to Assess Projects / Do you test the students?

On the first day I introduce the SL project, I distribute criteria for the project. As much as I can, I spell out the overall requirements. There is some flexibility regarding individual projects though. After choosing a project and meeting with the client, each team writes up a draft proposal for the project. Each team must keep minutes of all meetings and weekly report the team's progress. Each team must create a "deliverable" for the client and "publish" it. Each team member presents his or her work at a trade show conference we host at a local conference center. This is where they "publish," "announce,"— celebrate their work in and to the community. We invite the news service, the president, provost, and deans of the university, local officials, friends, faculty and staff, clients, of course, and other students. At the conclusion of the project, each team member submits a post project evaluation.

In addition to these assessment tools, I use the "Skills of Life," which business and industry have articulated to be essential to success in the workplace, as the basis of my midterm exam (See Figure 1 at the end of the chapter). I ask my students to reflect on their learning at midpoint in the semester in a well-organized essay. They are asked to choose and discuss four of the workplace skills and explain how they have incorporated these skills in the various activities, the project, and/or in the assignments in class. In the essay they also discuss the importance or   significance   of   using   these   skills.

For the final exam, I use the "tenets" of service learning as defined in the Clemson University Service Learning booklet (See Figure 2 at the end of the chapter). Just like the midterm exam, the final is in essay format, but this time, the students are asked to discuss the entire semester. Although we do much more in class than just the SL project over the course of a semester, most of the essays focus on the project. It could be because we spend the most time on it, but I know that it is because it is the one thing that has meant the most to the students.

The "Real" Benefits & Challenges for Service Learning

I will let my students speak. Jim says it best when he says, "I have learned that I don't just live in a college community, but that there is a larger community. I have always helped out in my hometown, but never thought about helping out here. I hope I can find the time to do more for this community." Brian, who was a bit of a cynic about the project said, "it is amazing the amount of mental energy that ignites itself when there is a reason to think." Stacy explains that "the date rape brochure showed [her] that each and every one of us can make a difference in the lives of others." Megan says that the most valuable thing about the SL project was "what [she] learned about [her]self and who [she] really is" while Michael learned that "the world did not revolve around just what [he] was interested in." Jason said that he had taken many classes during his four-year college career at Clemson, but "there has not been a class that has taught [him] so many useful skills for the real world and for citizenship." Many of the students also discussed the positive team experiences and the sense of accomplishment they felt upon presenting and completing their SL projects.

Conclusion

Service learning works. Service learning challenges and promotes students' personal, social, and intellectual growth. Through service learning, students develop civic responsibility, a sense of pride in work well done, and a sense of belonging to a team, a community, and a society. What other curriculum does all that?

Figure 1 Skills of Life Chart

This chart is adapted from a sheet that I received several years ago at a conference in Denver. After much discussion and debate, over 500 leaders from business, industry, and academics chose this list of skills necessary to succeed in life. It was also determined that schools from K-16 need to use these skills with their students so that students understand the "jargon" of work and show how they apply these skills in an academic setting.

Analyzing	Persuading
Appraising	Planning activities
Categorizing	Predicting
Communicating	Presenting
Computer word processing	Prioritizing
Conferring/conferencing	Reading
Counseling	Self-assessing
Estimating	Setting goals
Evaluating	Speaking
Following directions	Summarizing
Interviewing	Synthesizing
Investigating	Teaching/tutoring
Listening	Teaming with others
Managing time	Using computer databases
Negotiating	Using computer spreadsheets
Perceiving	Writing

Figure 2. "Tenets" of Clemson University Service Learning

❖ **Personal Growth** applies to the development of characteristics related to self-improvement and self-actualization.
- self-confidence and self esteem
- ability to take risks and accept challenges
- self understanding
- a sense of usefulness and purpose
- a sense of identity
- personal values and beliefs
- independence and autonomy
- self-respect

❖ **Social Growth** includes the social skills that are necessary for relating to others in society.
- communication skills
- a sense of belonging
- leadership skills
- peer team affiliation
- ability to work cooperatively with others
- a sense of caring for others
- acceptance and awareness of others from diverse and multicultural backgrounds

❖ **Intellectual Growth** encompasses the cognitive skills necessary to enhance academic learning and acquire higher level thinking skills.
- application of knowledge, relevance of curriculum
- problem solving and decision making skills
- critical thinking skills
- skills in learning from experience
- use of all learning styles
- development of a positive attitude toward learning

❖ **Citizenship** refers to the responsibilities of participation in a multicultural society and of citizenship in a democracy.
- a sense of responsibility to contribute to society
- democratic participation (informed citizen, exercises voting privileges)
- awareness of community needs

- organizational skills
- social action skills (persuasion, policy research, petitioning), empowerment, belief in ability to make a difference

❖ **Preparation for the World of Work** is the skills that help students gain work experience and make choices about possible career directions.

- human service skills
- realistic ideas about the world of work
- professionalism (dress, grooming, manners)
- ability to follow directions
- ability to function as a member of a team
- reliable working skills (punctuality, consistency, regular attendance) contacts and references for future job possibilities

Chapter Eight

Science

John R. Wagner and Erik R. Caldwell

Abstract

Elementary Education, Early Childhood Education, and Special Education majors at Clemson University are required to take a three-semester science sequence (physical science, earth science, and life science) specifically designed to model the teaching strategies they are expected to use later in their own classrooms. A variety of service learning formats and venues offers these future teachers the opportunity to interact with real elementary students engaged in meaningful science experiences in positive settings with structured reflection time. Students, instructors, and community clients report favorable results, however, some projects are more cost-effective and logistically manageable than others for large numbers of students.

Introduction

Each semester, at Clemson University, between 250 and 300 elementary, early childhood, and special education majors enroll in one of three science courses specifically designed for future teachers. PH

SC 107 (earth science), PH SC 108 (physical science), and BIOL 109 (life science) all model effective methods and strategies for teaching science to the targeted age group while covering critical science concepts recommended by various accrediting agencies and the National Science Teachers Association. I was a major instigator of the original curriculum restructuring plan to create a three-semester science sequence for these groups of preservice teachers. I designed and taught the pilot earth science course (PH SC 107) at Clemson in 1991 and 1992 and led a development team representing scientists, science educators, and inservice teachers in the design and implementation of the other two science courses with grant funding from the South Carolina Commission on Higher Education. All three courses were fully established and institutionalized at Clemson University by Fall Semester 1993.

One of the most important tenets of the restructured science sequence is the purposeful interaction of preservice teachers with practicing mentor teachers and the performance of science activities in actual elementary school classroom situations with actual elementary students. The involvement of successful elementary science teachers, in all aspects of our program, insures that these courses emphasize science concepts appropriate for 6-12 year olds and use only materials and supplies readily available to the average elementary school teacher.

I believe that a great deal of the credit for the success of the pilot course can be traced back to its service learning component. I gathered a wealth of research data from the pilot earth science course which indicated that preservice students left the course with a much improved attitude about science as well as improved confidence and understanding of major concepts (Wagner, Barbary, and Astwood, 1995). In the original grant program, we trained 24 local mentor teachers, and assigned each of them six Clemson students from the course. Following a series of meetings, these 144 students observed science classes at the mentor teacher's school, worked out a science activity especially for that grade level, and presented the activity both in the elementary classroom and at an after-school "homework center." The responses to both the mentoring and the field experiences were very positive. The mentor teachers enjoyed working with the Clemson students, the elementary children were thrilled to do some exciting science activities with a "visiting" teacher, and the Clemson students appreciated the chance for "real-life" encounters in the classroom.

Unfortunately, the full service learning component was never successfully integrated into the three courses. While every student enrolled had contact with real elementary students in either a classroom or non-classroom setting at some point during the semester, once grant funding ended, resources dried up and the scope of the service learning projects had to be scaled back considerably as new course instructors discovered they had insufficient time to supervise that large a number of students and also arrange contacts with schools and other community organizations. Furthermore, the demise of the College of Sciences during university restructuring and the subsequent assignment of the physical and biological science departments into separate colleges made coordination of the three courses more difficult. The life science outreach program died first, and after several years of diminishing student participation, even the highly diluted service learning component of the physical science and earth science courses was in danger of disappearing.

The establishment of the Clemson University Service Learning Collaborative in 1997 focused attention on all colleges to consider ways of incorporating service learning into their courses. The Department of Geological Sciences was aware of my previous success with this type of outreach program in the courses for elementary education majors and asked me to determine what it would take to once again provide a full complement of service learning experiences for both the physical science and earth science courses. I met several times with the instructor for those courses, Rick White, who supported the service learning component in principle. Together we raised and explored possible implementation options with the Service Learning Collaborative.

As a result of this groundwork, Rick White and I submitted a proposal and received a mini-grant for the 1998 Spring Semester to develop a sustainable service learning program for the physical science and earth science courses. The intent was to test a variety of service learning project formats to determine which ones were both cost effective and time effective and also logistically manageable for classes of up to 150 introductory students. By hiring a part-time Service Learning Coordinator, we were able to reinstate a full program of service learning experiences for all students enrolled in PH SC 107 and PH SC 108 during the Spring 1998 Semester. Erik Caldwell, a graduate of Clemson's hydrogeology masters program who also had an interest in teaching, agreed to work with us as Coordinator. His job was to initiate, implement, and monitor as wide a variety of service learning projects as possible to determine which would be sustainable under anticipated levels of departmental and college support. The Department of Geological Sciences agreed to allocate one-third of a Graduate Teaching Assistant position to maintain the service learning emphasis in future semesters and also agreed to provide funding for necessary materials and supplies.

The Service Learning Project

Laying the Groundwork

Early in January of 1998, Erik Caldwell began planning and organizing a number of potential service learning opportunities for the physical science and earth science courses to be offered in the Spring 1998 Semester. Erik was responsible for initiating all institutional contacts and arranging schedules and other logistical details for each category and format of service learning project, including those involving direct involvement with elementary school classes. We had been repeatedly cautioned by public school representatives and by colleagues in Clemson's School of Education that our students should not be permitted to contact teachers directly. I supported their position because I could imagine the chaos that would be unleashed at our local elementary school if 200 Clemson students decided to start contacting teachers independently and randomly at the beginning of our Spring Semester in January.

Erik took advantage of many of the institutional contacts we had cultivated previously during the time of grant sponsorship. He also scouted out additional resources in the Clemson area and enlisted help from the National Dropout Prevention Center, which had provided the original catalyst for the formation of the Clemson Service Learning Collaborative, and the Anderson-Oconee-Pickens Science and Math Hub, one of thirteen state sponsored education resource offices in South Carolina. Both of those agencies are headquartered on the Clemson University campus and both were willing to help identify potential service learning projects that would be suitable for our students and also of value to the community.

Erik presented his list of potential formats and venues to me and Rick White. We compiled a list of acceptable service learning projects in which our students could participate. Our basic criteria for selecting projects stipulated that they be of service to the community, be educational in nature, relate to the physical science (or earth science) class curriculum if possible, and provide a diverse range of age groups, settings, and schedule times for the Clemson students to select from.

Our final list of approved service learning venues included: after-school homework centers at four nearby elementary schools; the Geology Museum at Clemson University, which receives visits from dozens of school groups each month; the Clemson Montessori School; meetings of local 4-H Clubs and Cub Scout troops; evening sessions of the Family Math and Science Program run through the Anderson-Oconee-Pickens Hub; local elementary classrooms using science kits prepared by the Hub; Saturday children's programs and public tours sponsored by the South Carolina Botanical Gardens, also located on the Clemson campus; a department based "ask-a-scientist" outreach center, where elementary school children could send in questions they wanted answered; and a few additional customized projects that were designed specifically to address scheduling problems or other special circumstances of individual students (see Figure 1).

Many service learning assignments require student groups to identify and analyze a community problem before selecting an agency to collaborate with and planning their strategy for addressing the issue. Because of our large number of students, and the fact that most of them were freshmen taking an introductory course, we thought it would be preferable, and certainly more manageable, to pre-select the sites and times. Once this was done, Erik prepared a matrix showing all possible combinations of time, place, and site and then assigned groups of students to each one. It is important to note that although Erik made all the logistical arrangements for where and when each service learning experience would take place, it was still the students' responsibility to determine, in consultation with the institutional representative, exactly what type of activity they would plan for the elementary children with whom they would be interacting.

At this point, we needed to set up a formal mechanism to incorporate the service learning experience into both the physical science and earth science course curricula. Erik and I met with course instructor Rick White to discuss how this project should appear on the course syllabus and how it should be graded. We determined that counting the service learning grade as 5% of the total course grade was consistent with our expectations of time expenditure (about 10 hours worth of work) and was a high enough percentage so that even uninterested students would have to take the project seriously. Our overall goal was to raise the level of student understanding about service learning as well as to instill positive attitudes about the experience and have them regard the experience as a natural extension of their course content. To insure that our students knew what was expected of them, we prepared a one-page handout (Figure 2) that was distributed at the same time as the project assignments.

We expected that the biggest logistical hurdle in managing nearly 200 students would be matching student schedules with available project times. So rather than ask students to immediately select a preferred format or venue, we decided instead to circulate a sign-up sheet with five time intervals: morning (from 9-12); early afternoon (from 12-3); late afternoon (from 3-6); evening (from 6-9); and Saturdays. Each student indicated their first and second choice of times, and Erik then collected the schedules and grouped the students into teams of four, based on their time selection, and placed them into service learning activities that could be completed during the times they selected (Figure 3). In some time frames, such as afternoons, there were several project formats for students to be assigned to; in others, like Saturdays, only one was possible.

Preparation

We decided to formally introduce the basic concepts of service learning during a class lecture period early in the semester. Erik recruited Scott Brown from the National Dropout Prevention Center and Dr. Brenda Vander Mey, a sociologist from Clemson University, to deliver a 15 minute introduction to the topic. These guest speakers presented the major goals and objectives of service learning and explained the standard framework of 'preparation', 'action', 'reflection', and 'celebration'. We thought that an external presenter would have more credibility on this topic than the course instructor and we wanted to impress upon the students that service learning is much more than just a required activity of their science course.

After the introductory 15 minute lecture, the class split off into different classrooms based on their assigned project groups. Even though we had posted the group assignments earlier, several students had forgotten which group they belonged to, which created some confusion and delay in getting everybody into the right place. Once that issue was resolved, representatives of the different community groups and agencies gave our students some background information on the agency and the children with whom they would be working. Each presenter outlined the parameters under which the service learning project would be conducted and any specific issues the students would have to be aware of as they did their planning. We were concerned that each student understand exactly what was expected of them as well as what support they could expect from the participating agency, and any dress codes, activity restrictions, etc. that might be in force.

Erik recruited volunteers from most of the project venues to come to Clemson that day and meet with the student groups who were to work with their programs. Because elementary schools were in session at the time our college classes met, it was not feasible to bring in teachers, so I met with the Clemson students who had been assigned to homework centers, staff from the Anderson-Oconee-Pickens Science Hub met with students who were to do Family Science and the Science Kits in classrooms, and Erik Caldwell met with students assigned to the Montessori School and the 'question and answer' project.

While it might have been preferable to allow each student group to visit each project venue separately and determine for themselves what type of interaction with elementary students would be most beneficial to both groups, the sheer numbers of students in our classes led us to take a different approach. For each service learning venue that Erik had identified, he spoke to an administrator and/or resource person to determine first if there was a need for service, and second what types of activities would best fit the needs of the agency. For the most part, their responses fit well into the framework we had set up. Most of the projects provided clear opportunities for our students to incorporate their physical science or earth science coursework. An obvious example is the Geology Museum, to which Erik assigned only earth science students.

After the students concluded their initial meeting with their assigned agency representative, they met in groups, independently, several times to devise a plan of action which they thought would best address the issues raised at the initial meeting. When the group thought its plan was complete, they scheduled a meeting with Erik to have it approved before putting it into action. Depending on the quality of their plan, Erik would either approve it as presented, approve it with certain modifications, or ask the students to explore some different approaches and bring back a revised plan at a later date. Most formats and venues also required additional meetings with site representatives before the project plan was put into action. All student groups were required to plan for and arrange their own transportation to the service learning project location.

Action

The homework centers that Erik dealt with, Morrison Elementary in Clemson, Pendleton Elementary in Pendleton, Ravenel Elementary in Seneca, and Code Elementary in Seneca, all said they needed as much help as we could send. Almost half of our students, 78 out of 194, were assigned to one of these four centers. At the initial information session, our students were advised to plan for one of two types of activities; either tutoring (basically helping the students complete their science homework), or leading some type of hands-on science activity with a subset of the children at the center. Student teams were permitted to decide which approach to take with the proviso that tutoring required at least four visits (from 2:45 PM - 4:00 PM on certain days) and the hands-on presentation required at least one visit at a time mutually agreeable to the team and the center. Groups that selected the latter option were expected to meet independently several times prior to their presentation in order to organize and rehearse their performance and gather the necessary materials and supplies. The directors of each homework center were responsible for supervising our students' activities and conveying feedback to Erik Caldwell.

The Geology Museum's primary need was for volunteers to help conduct tours for visiting classes of elementary school students. About 30 of our students were assigned to this project. Planning for this activity required each student group to meet with coordinator Rick White at least two times, for a total of two hours, to learn about the museum and its contents and be trained in strategies of traffic control and tour management. Once trained, the student groups met two or three times with classes of elementary school students at the museum and essentially ran the tour. Each student in the group took charge of from five to ten elementary school children, showing them around the museum in the allotted time. Our students focused on answering the children's questions, imparting basic geologic information to them, and entertaining them. The children also received a souvenir rock after their visit was complete.

Only one group, composed of four physical science students, was assigned to the Montessori School in Clemson. The school was willing to take many more students, but their early morning time frame was not a popular option for our students. This group was scheduled for two sessions for two hours each time. They worked with fourth and fifth graders, helping in the classroom. Erik had arranged for them to contact the head of the Montessori School to arrange a time for orientation, which was to last about one hour. Once the orientation was complete, the students could then arrange the other two meetings with the school. Montessori schools have a different teaching methodology. The school encourages the children to move at their own pace with the teachers guiding them along. We selected this venue as an option for our students because we thought they should be exposed to as many different educational philosophies as possible.

Two groups, totaling eight students, originally were assigned to work with two local 4-H clubs. One group contacted a 4-H club located in the town of Due West, SC. The other 4-H club was unable to accommodate our time constraints, but Erik was able at the last minute to arrange for the second group to do their project with a Cub Scout den. In each case, Erik provided our students with the necessary contact information and allowed them to arrange the time, place and details of the presentation. Although the project required only one meeting with the children, student groups were to meet independently prior to that date to rehearse their presentation and gather necessary materials and supplies. Erik made it clear that he was to be kept informed about the details and would have to approve the subject of the activity.

Central Elementary School in Pickens County and Ravenel Elementary School in Oconee County conducted a series of evening Family Math and Science activities in late February and early March. These sessions were organized with the help of the Anderson-Oconee-Pickens Science and Math Hub, which is charged with fostering increased interaction among schools, parents, and children, in addition to its many other professional development tasks. The Family Science and Math Initiative is part of a national effort to provide opportunities for learning outside of the traditional classroom setting. Erik arranged for a total of eight groups, of four students each, to participate in these evening sessions. Each group had to attend two sessions, each visit lasting about two hours, in addition to meeting in groups ahead of time to prepare for the event. During the visits our students assisted school personnel with set-up and take-down, and individually helped participants in their efforts to understand and enjoy the designated activities. They also answered a variety of questions that came up, not only about the activity itself, but about science concepts in general.

Erik arranged for four groups, a total of 16 students, to help introduce the use of science kits in several local elementary school classrooms. Our students first learned about the Science Kits and their use from meetings with staff from the Anderson-Oconee-Pickens Science and Math Hub. The Hub has worked extensively with kit-based science and has developed several modules to help teachers teach science in the elementary classroom. Erik assigned each student group to a specific school, which they visited a total of four times to assist the teachers participating in the Hub program. The teachers scheduled the use of the science kits in the early afternoon for about an hour and a half each time. The elementary schools that participated in this activity were Ravenel Elementary and James Brown Elementary in Oconee County, and Morrison Elementary in Pickens County,. The teachers in these schools expressed great interest in having our students come help in their classrooms. Erik had stressed to our students that they were there not just to observe the science kit activity, but also to participate actively. Each of our students served as facilitator/resource person for a group of elementary students during the activity.

In late February and early March the South Carolina Botanical Garden, located on the Clemson campus, scheduled a special series of Science Saturday events to coincide with their regularly scheduled Saturday public walks and tours. The Science Saturday program was designed for elementary school kids and their families and was intended to attract new visitors to the Botanical Garden. Erik arranged to send about 40 of our students, in groups, to help with these special events. We were warned that, due to weather considerations and unpredictable visitor turnout, it might be difficult to guarantee that all of our students would have first-hand contact with children. However we agreed that, even with a low public turnout, our students could still assist the staff and enjoy a quality service learning experience. Each Saturday session lasted about three hours, from 9 am until about 12 noon, and each of our student groups was required to meet with staff from the Botanical Garden the preceding Thursday for an orientation session.

The most flexible service learning format was the question and answer project. Eight students were assigned to this group and they were given free reign as to when and how they would complete the project. They read through and discussed a set of written questions submitted by elementary school children and sent them a written response. The idea for this particular project originated from a pile of science questions that I had received from a elementary school class in the lower part of the state over the Christmas holidays and had not had time to answer. Our students also contacted several local teachers to solicit additional questions from children in their classes. In addition to the time spent writing responses, our students had to spend time researching the question and discussing with each other the best way to phrase their answers so that the children would understand the concept. The question and answer project gave the children practice in formulating written questions while also teaching our future elementary teachers how to write responses that answer science questions at an age appropriate level.

In a couple of instances, students came to Erik with a specific idea for their own project and time frame. As long as their plan met the service learning requirements that we used to validate the other group activities, we let them do it as individuals. We also had one or two cases in which students had signed up for time slots that turned out to be impossible for them to actually schedule with the rest of their group. In these situations, we reluctantly agreed that the affected student could carry out their project alone, without the participation of the rest of their group. Such customized service learning projects worked well, but required Erik to spend much more time with these individuals than with the average student.

Reflection

Each of the service learning projects assigned in the physical science and earth science courses contained several built-in opportunities for reflection, some of them required and graded, others simply recommended. The first occurred immediately after the in-class meeting of student groups with representatives from community agencies. At that session, each group was urged to get together as soon as possible to discuss among themselves their individual expectations and concerns about their upcoming assignment. We had no official mechanism for monitoring student compliance with this request, but Service Learning Coordinator Erik Caldwell suspected that most groups did pursue this task based on the comments they submitted to him with their plan of action. The scheduled group meeting with Erik also gave him the opportunity to raise issues the group had overlooked and to reinforce the importance of critically evaluating one's own service experience, especially in those venues with multiple sessions, so that our students could learn from their encounter and improve their performance in future sessions.

The first formal reflection assignment was due immediately following each group's first project activity session. Erik outlined the criteria for this report on the 'Service Learning Project' handout given to both classes (Figure 2). Each group was to submit a reflective report (as opposed to three or four individual reports) which critically reviewed the group's first service experience and suggested changes in procedures or strategies for future encounters. Groups involved in projects with multiple sessions were required to submit a group reflective report after each scheduled event. These reports were submitted via e-mail to Erik, who confirmed receipt and responded with comments and suggestions when appropriate. We did not grade these reports except to record them as 'completed' or 'not completed'.

The final reflective assignment consisted of a typed narrative report, no more than a couple pages long, which briefly summarized the entire project and the various aspects of the reflection process. Erik reviewed each report and assigned it a grade of 'complete', 'partially complete', or 'incomplete'. The assignment instructions stressed the importance of including a subjective analysis of the service learning experience, as well as the standard objective data.

Celebration

The celebration component of the service learning framework was certainly our weakest link. We had planned to design special certificates to hand out on the last day of class to those who had successfully completed the service learning assignment, but we were never able to set aside the time necessary for preparation and printing. Recognition, for most of our students, came solely through spontaneously gestures from the site organizers or from the elementary children themselves through thank-you notes, small tokens of appreciation, and local media coverage promoted by the community agency. It is important to note that we did not intentionally prompt any of the community recognition, even though we believe we should have. It is also significant that many students stated in their final project reports that the service learning experience was 'rewarding', even though they did not receive any external token of recognition.

We did confer special recognition on a few students who performed exceptionally well in their role as geology museum tour guides. We asked these students to take part in filming a service learning videotape that the Clemson Service Learning Collaborative was producing. We filmed these students leading a special museum tour with children, then interviewed each of them to get their perceptions of what the service learning experience had meant to them. We also invited these same students to speak at a special one-day service learning conference sponsored by the Collaborative.

Results

The hiring of a Service Learning Coordinator was extremely successful in making the assignments practical and manageable for such large lecture sections of introductory science students. The vast majority of community organizations that were contacted responded favorably to our invitation to participate in a service learning venture and were willing to send a representative to talk to a subset of the science class. The class session devoted to service learning was well received, even though the students were somewhat apprehensive about the assignment. Getting the student groups into their respective room assignments to meet with the community representatives was more difficult than expected because many students had forgotten which group they had signed up for.

Once the students had been introduced to their project, they were essentially on their own to make additional community contacts and schedule their own group meetings. They were told to contact Service Learning Coordinator Erik Caldwell if they experienced any problems. The class handouts they had been given contained the appropriate deadlines and other information needed to plan the service learning project. No attempt was made to force the students to meet with Erik.

This was done intentionally to place as much responsibility on the students as possible.

Unfortunately, many groups took advantage of this apparent lack of structure to procrastinate and did not contact Erik until the posted deadlines. As a result, he spent an average of three hours per day, from the end of February to the middle of March, answering e-mail, arranging meetings, and dealing with questions about service learning from almost 200 students. However, almost all of the students eventually did come in their groups to see him or sent a group representative to meet with him. Two groups arranged their entire project through e-mail.

In general, Erik gave each group the information it needed to start its project. This included contact details, directions to the location where they were going, what they were going to do when they got there, and the objectives of their project from the point of view of the community sponsor. Groups that had a strong leader and active participants seemed to have little difficulty in organizing and carrying out their project plan. Some groups, however, lacked a natural leader and/or contained marginally active students who missed group meetings and even some scheduled activities. In many of these cases, Erik was not informed about the problems until it was too late to do anything to resolve them successfully.

The most difficult part of this project was the monitoring of the actual service learning activities. In most cases we had to rely on the community leaders and school teachers and administrators just to determine whether the student groups had shown up on time and successfully completed their activity. This was an especially difficult problem with the large number of students assigned to the homework centers. The other activities were small enough in scope and centralized enough that it was not as difficult to monitor them. With so many students involved in nine different activities, some trust must be assumed. We considered the feasibility of using sign-in sheets to help monitor student attendance, but decided against it because we thought it might create a logistical nightmare in terms of delivering and picking up paperwork. Undoubtedly we received a few reports from groups that never actually performed the activities they described, but Erik, who read all of the reports and received feedback from all of the project sites, believes that the vast majority of reports were truthful.

Feedback from student reports and from the community sponsors indicated that all of the activities except for the tutoring at homework centers were appropriate experiences and met most if not all of our service learning criteria. The homework centers certainly needed volunteers, but most of the tutoring work done by our student teams did not involve the science content we were addressing in the college courses. The majority of our students complained that the subjects they helped most with were spelling, math and reading. In general, the students said the tutoring experience was rewarding but it did not complement their course curriculum.

Although the reflective report(s) and the final report were submitted by teams, not by individuals, the grades reported to course instructor Rick White did contain individual variations due to some students being penalized for not showing up for presentations. The other team members were not penalized in these cases, only the guilty party. The entire project was worth 50 points. The average grade was 40. The median grade was somewhat higher, because a few teams, which never completed their project and therefore received a grade of 0, pulled down the class average but not the median.

Planned and Unplanned Outcomes

We had purposely designed our service learning projects for groups of four students to plan and carry out because of the current research emphasis on cooperative learning as an effective pedagogical tool at all grade levels, but also because the thought of monitoring and grading the performance of nearly 200 students individually was too daunting a task to contemplate. We expected these education majors to be somewhat familiar with group work, but learned that the majority of our freshman students had no idea what a cooperative learning group was or how it functioned. When team members already knew each other personally, the system worked well. But teams that were randomly assigned rarely functioned well, primarily because no one took charge. In some cases this situation soured the opinion of group members towards the project.

Our expectation, which was articulated in class during the initial lecture introducing service learning, was that the group would meet and select its leader. However, without a designated leader to call a meeting, many groups never met at all. In a freshman course with large enrollments, the distribution of students into groups will likely continue to be a problem unless group roles are clearly assigned at the beginning of the project and the entire group is held responsible for the performance of all its members. By contrast, in a smaller class setting where the team members already could have spent some time working together, thereby developing a better rapport, we believe the team focus would have proven to be a much more effective strategy.

There were two main categories of problems encountered with the service learning venues recruited for this project. The first type of problem involved students complaining about scheduling conflicts. Despite all our efforts to place people in appropriate time slots that they themselves had selected, many team members later discovered scheduling conflicts either with other team members or with the community group. This problem necessitated many last minute personnel changes among teams and rescheduling of activities. In some instances we gave students who had scheduling conflicts with their other team members permission to do the project on their own. Perhaps a policy of posting a list of available times and venues and allowing students to form their own groups and sign up for projects would help, but it would not alleviate the problem of freshmen in a large introductory course not knowing many of their fellow students or their schedules.

The second problem was the inflexibility of certain site directors and the inappropriateness of some of the activities our students were asked to perform. For example, we thought, from previous experience, that the after-school homework centers would be the perfect place for a team of students to present an interactive science lesson, do an experiment, or set up a demonstration for the children. However, one of our homework centers withdrew its support for our hands-on science activities because they believed the center's primary mission was to help students complete their homework, and that the children simply did not have time for extra activities. Several of our student groups were confronted with this dilemma after they had already agreed to work with that center. Erik recommended that they contact other homework centers that had already accommodated several of our student groups, and assure the director that the activity would be done only after the children had completed their homework. Many of our students in this situation did not complete their project because they were either unable or unwilling to contact other homework centers.

Most of the project formats did not require much additional attention once Erik had given the students the appropriate instructions, however, the geology museum was an exception. Course instructor Rick White was asked to train the students that were going to conduct tours of the geology museum for visiting school children. Scheduling again was a major problem as Rick had to run several additional training sessions for students who had missed their assigned times. He reported that the total time spent training, scheduling and overseeing the tours was close to 20 hours for only 32 students. This level of time commitment is obviously too high for a full time faculty member, or even for a graduate student helper. Continued use of the museum as a service learning site will depend on finding a less time-intensive method for training students.

The use of e-mail was time consuming, but much more time-effective than face-to-face meetings would have been. On the whole it proved to be a very efficient and simple way to communicate. Even receiving a total of four to five e-mail messages from up to 200 students over the course of a semester should not pose a major problem. Erik was very pleased with the performance of the e-mail system and somewhat surprised that our students were as familiar with it as they were. He received messages from close to 90 percent of the students enrolled in the physical science and earth science courses and reports that it was easy for him to respond at his leisure.

One final important unexpected outcome was the pledge of future financial support for service learning from the Department of Geological Sciences. After having our program successes praised and publicized by the Clemson Service Learning Collaborative, both the department and the college expressed a desire to continue the service learning component, in both the earth science and physical science courses, for future semesters. They agreed to provide the same level of funding each semester that the Service Learning Collaborative had provided for the pilot program.

Evaluation

Evaluation is a multi-faceted process. The overall quality of student performance was evaluated primarily by Service Learning Coordinator Erik Caldwell in a holistic manner, incorporating his personal assessment of student participation, the reflective and final reports, feedback from the site-based directors, and consideration of any missed meetings or activity sessions. These factors were all combined and reported as individual numerical student grades and passed along to course instructor Rick White to be averaged in with grades of exams and other course assignments.

Grading of projects was by nature subjective and was complicated by factors such as: students only showing up once or twice when they were supposed to go to a site three times; students missing their assigned activity time because of faulty communication; some team members not attending all meetings; a group waiting to the last minute to define a project, etc. Most of the students seemed to care more about their grade than they did about the philosophy of the project. Discounting individual negative circumstances, any team that completed its project and sent e-mail reports as directed received a project grade of either 40 or 50 points out of 50, depending on the completeness of their written reports. Those teams partially completing their project received between 25 and 35 points, depending on receipt of e-mail and completeness of their written reports. Those not doing the project at all received no points.

Evaluating the usefulness of each different community service format for our students was also an important consideration. One of our project goals was to determine which venues provided the most effective and efficient mechanisms for incorporating a sustainable service learning component into the earth science and life science courses. Service Learning Coordinator Erik Caldwell kept track of the number of hours he spent dealing with each different format and project type during the semester. We also tabulated student comments from reflective and final reports and weighed anecdotal comments about the appropriateness of each category of project. We were able to determine that major problems existed with some homework centers and with the geology museum. All other formats appeared to work well with our constituency.

Evaluating the effectiveness of the project as a whole required feedback both from our students and from local site directors. Responses from both groups were overwhelmingly positive indicating that the service learning project was a success. Most students responded favorably to the project, many wrote that it was much better than they expected. But some students felt that this type of project should be announced before they had even signed up for the class, believing that a project of this magnitude was unfair to spring on them at the beginning of the semester. Several of the community leaders commented on how much they enjoyed the students and their help.

Typical comments received from evaluation forms include: "I've thoroughly enjoyed working with these [Clemson] students! Their knowledge and their rapport with the students have been impressive." (mentor teacher); "I enjoyed forming my own science lab, and I especially loved watching it run successfully. The children were a complete joy to work with. They reminded me once again that being a teacher is both wonderful and rewarding." (Clemson student); "I have always had a negative feeling towards science and I thought it would be hard to teach the lesson. But as I went through the lesson, I saw how much fun it was. I can't wait to have a classroom of my own." (Clemson student). A few students realized that they really weren't cut out to be teachers and are considering changing their major. It is preferable that such students discover this fact early in their college career.

Benefits and Challenges

Duckenfield and Wright (1995) define service learning as a "teaching/learning method that connects meaningful community service with academic scholarship, civic responsibility, and personal enrichment." Aside from the obvious benefits of providing knowledgeable volunteers to community agencies and schools, service learning also enhances the learning process for college students by providing opportunities for the practical application of academic theory. It provides students with a framework for planning, acting, reflecting and celebrating opportunities to help the community, and also develops social skills they will need later in their academic career. The need for preservice teachers to be well versed in doing service learning is of critical importance if their future students are to be encouraged in similar pursuits.

Service learning experiences should be an integral part of the curriculum for elementary education, early childhood education, and special education majors. In addition to the personal benefits to these future teachers, there are strong professional reasons why service learning should be incorporated into their course of study. Elementary school children in particular have always been encouraged to become involved in community service through their schools, whether it be in newspaper drives, recycling efforts, UNICEF collections at Halloween, or clean-up/paint-up projects. To effectively lead such projects, future teachers should have had personal experience participating in similar efforts.

Science classes provide an ideal platform in which to model service learning because so many community projects are related to science in some way. The science sequence required of elementary education, early childhood education, and special education majors (PH SC 107, PH SC 108, BIOL 109) was designed to model effective science teaching strategies in hopes that these students would eventually teach their own classes in the same way they were taught at Clemson. Including service learning activities within these courses sends the message that such community building activities should also be included.

In many teacher preparation programs, rising teachers only have contact with students in a passive role as observers for the first few semesters of their undergraduate career. This passive contact with students is seen as a weakness by most science educators and service learning is viewed as a possible solution to providing more active contact between student teachers and the children in their classrooms. For most undergraduate students, waiting until their senior year to find out they don't like teaching, working with, or supervising elementary students is too late for a reasonable change of career plans. Giving the Clemson science students early contact with elementary school students in a positive setting with structured reflective time is one of the major objectives the service learning program was designed to accomplish.

Summary and Conclusion

It is possible to incorporate a successful service learning component into a high enrollment, introductory undergraduate science course at a major research university. The critical factor is the availability of a Service Learning Coordinator to manage the logistical arrangements and keep records of student performance. We hired a Visiting Instructor to serve this function at Clemson during Spring Semester 1998, but a graduate student, or a very capable undergraduate student, or perhaps even a local retired person could serve equally well, as long as they were familiar with the community and with service opportunities in the local area.

Some modifications to the standard service learning framework may be necessary to accommodate the large numbers of students. The most obvious restriction is that our students did not have as much freedom to investigate and define their own service activity as we might have liked. Another restriction we imposed was the four-person group structure in which we arbitrarily assigned student teams to service learning venues based on time and schedule preferences. We also insisted that they obtain approval for their plan from our Service Learning Coordinator instead of negotiating directly with the local site director. We felt such restrictions were necessary to avoid overloading the capability of the site directors to deal with the very large numbers of volunteers.

The vast majority of the work of the Service Learning Coordinator occurs early in the semester and involves the organization of all of the logistical arrangements. It is critical that the service learning venues offered are ones that can be utilized efficiently and effectively with large numbers of students. Once student groups receive their assignment and have their plan of action approved, the Coordinator's job becomes one of monitoring student progress for the remainder of the semester. Grading of student reports can also be a major time consuming task.

We believe that our service learning initiative met most of the goals and objectives we established for our program. Our students planned, implemented and evaluated a worthwhile, class-related activity outside of the classroom. For many of them, this was their first contact with children in an educational setting. Many students were reassured about their career choice after participating. Others decided that classroom teaching wasn't for them. The commitment of departmental support has insured that the service learning component will continue as an integral part of the pre-service science courses at Clemson University.

Figure 1. Categories of Service Learning Projects Used in Spring 1998

Category	Venue	Time Schedule	Sponsor
Homework Centers	local elementary schools	late afternoons	local elementary schools
Geology Museum	Clemson University campus	early afternoons	Clemson Department of Geological Sciences
Montessori School	local Clemson school	early mornings	Clemson Montessori School
4-H / Cub Scouts	Troop meetings in Due West and Clemson	evenings	4-H / Cub Scouts
Family Science	local elementary schools	evenings	Anderson-Oconee-Pickens Science and Math Hub
Science Kits	local elementary schools	early afternoons	Anderson-Oconee-Pickens Science and Math Hub
Science Saturday	Botanical Garden Clemson University	Saturday mornings	South Carolina Botanical Garden
Question and Answer	Clemson University campus	variable	Clemson Department of Geological Sciences
Customized Projects	variable	variable	variable

Figure 3. Distribution of Clemson Student Participants and Elementary Student Participants by Category of Service Learning Project

Category	# Clemson Students	# Participating Children
Homework Centers	78	120
Geology Museum	27	320
Montessori Schools	4	20
4-H / Cub Scouts	7	30
Family Science	16	40
Science Kits	13	90
Science Saturday	32	15
Question and Answer	15	80
Customized Projects	2	10
TOTAL	**194**	**725**

Figure 2. Class Handout Explaining Service Learning Project Tasks

---

Service Learning Project

What is service learning?

Service learning provides students with the opportunity to participate in thoughtfully organized service experiences that meet community needs. Service learning is integrated into the course curriculum and provides time for the expression and evaluation of the experience. Service learning enhances classroom education by involving hands-on learning, beneficial service, and application of academic skills outside of the classroom.

Benefits to participating students include: improved self-confidence, independence, and responsibility. Students have opportunities to improve communication, leadership and organizational skills as well as utilize classroom knowledge, experiential education, and critical thinking skills in fulfilling a community need.

Procedure

You will need to plan, do, and evaluate your service activity. The planning will be done as a team with Erik Caldwell. You will need to schedule a time to meet with Erik to discuss your plan. (See schedule below for deadlines) Once the plan has been approved you can then implement the plan. After each time you meet on this activity the team will submit a *reflective report*.

In this report the following items will be addressed: Who? Where? When? What? ('What' will involve: what was done, what did you plan, etc.) Why? ('Why' will include: why was the activity done, why your activity did/didn't work, etc.) How? ('How' will include: how was the activity, how could it be improved next time, etc.). These reports will be submitted to Erik Caldwell by e-mail <**caldwel@clemson.edu**>.

A written (**not e-mail**) one page, typed final report encompassing the total experience will need to be submitted by the 20th of April. It should include the above elements and address your group's overall feeling about the project. Only one report per group is to be turned in.

Evaluation

This project is worth 5% of your overall grade. The amount of total time spent on this project should be between 10-12 hours. The grade will be assigned holistically and will include evaluation of: participation, reflection, and reports from the site coordinators/administrators.

Works Cited

Wagner, J.R., Barbary, S.W., and Astwood, P.M., "Full Circle Partnerships for Elementary Science Education: A Collaborative Approach to Group Learning in Earth Science," *Journal of Geological Education* , *43*, 376-380 (1995).

Duckenfield, M. and Wright, J. [eds.], *Pocket Guide to Service Learning* , National Dropout Prevention Center - Clemson University (1995).

Chapter Nine

Education

Carol G. Weatherford & Emma M. Owens

Abstract

Service learning is coming into its own. Teacher Education programs traditionally have been slow to adopt and maintain teaching methodologies that take the learning process outside the walls of the schools. Service learning connects classroom learning with real life experiences. This chapter discusses how pre-service teachers are provided opportunities to experience service learning as a valuable teaching tool. This chapter also chronicles the growth and development of the authors' adaptations of the methodology. Applying classroom learning to real classrooms and real students is an important goal of teacher education programs. At Clemson University, professors in the teacher education program have increasingly utilized service learning as a methodology that links classroom learning with real world experiences and expectations. Even before coming into the professional education program, while taking general education courses, some students have service learning opportunities related to teaching and learning.

Introduction

In this chapter, we will discuss why service learning as a methodology is needed in pre-service teacher education and describe how several faculty members have integrated service learning into the teacher education curricula. We will also describe our vision of what teacher education could look like in relation to service learning. Although the focus of this chapter is to describe how service learning has been integrated into the pre-service teacher education program, service learning has also been introduced into the graduate program as a three-hour Master's level course for in-service teachers. In addition, two completed doctoral dissertations and at least two other dissertations in progress in Curriculum and Instruction have studied service learning or related topics.

Service learning provides a method to challenge students in teacher education who, for the most part, have lived and known a middle-class life style. Most teacher education students at Clemson University have been reared by two-parent families and many students come from families with at least one grandparent having completed a college education. Therefore, much of the current pre-service teaching force views the students in their classroom through rose-colored lenses. They measure future students and the families of future students against their own middle-class standards. Their understanding of the real life experiences of many of the students who will be in their classrooms is limited by the homogeneity of their experiences. Service learning provides a hands-on opportunity for pre-service teacher educators to learn to value diversity and to appreciate the contributions and strengths of others whom they may not have always held in high esteem because they are operating without knowledge and have not had the advantage of interacting with people who come from different backgrounds. The lessons learned from serving students who have different experiences from their own increase their future effectiveness as teachers while providing needed services for students and their families.

Through service learning, students also have opportunities to learn how to connect community resources with the needs of students and families. Areas of personal needs which teachers often encounter in classrooms include warm clothing, shoes, socks, school supplies, age-appropriate reading materials, techniques and strategies for addressing the problem of head lice and other health and environmental concerns as well as vision exams and prescription glasses.

Service learning experiences have been integrated into all levels of field experiences for pre-service teacher education students at Clemson University. Entering students, sophomores, juniors, and seniors have opportunities for service learning.

Level One

In the initial field experience, *Orientation to the Profession* , which enrolls 300 students per semester, service learning is introduced as a method of integrating curricula areas and life's lessons together. As an alternative to the more traditional approach of teaching subjects in separate time frames, the service learning method captures the meaning of students' learning as a unified whole and offers students the option of working in teams rather than in isolation. For the *Orientation to the Profession* field experience, students are placed primarily in a single school district which coordinates tutoring opportunities across the district in elementary, middle, and secondary schools, in regular and in special education classes, and in some after school programs. In addition, after school programs in community settings offer learning sites for pre-service teachers who are interested in meeting the needs of those particular sites. The course instructor has indicated that because of service learning, she has learned new ways to enthuse students and that it is important to give students experiences that excite them about what they can do rather than emphasize what they cannot do. In addition, she has identified the following major outcomes from students' service learning experiences: students develop an appreciation for contributions and learn that contributing is a two-way street; teaching is not just having students answer the questions at the end of the chapter but is an integrative, reflective process which involves the whole person; service learning helps students become more visionary and to think 'outside the box'; students also learn that they do not just teach a particular subject in an hour. The instructor sums up her experience with service learning by stating, "What the students have learned, I've learned, too."

Level Two

In the sophomore field experience that is part of the course *Child Growth and Development*, students implement some of the instructional ideas generated in their class with children in public school settings. In order to accomplish this goal, students utilize the service learning framework: preparation, action, reflection and celebration. Students identify a need, which is a major part of preparation, by utilizing one of several methods learned as part of the class. The course textbook is used as a resource to identify developmental needs of children, which may or may not be verified by additional, more localized information provided through *Kids Count Data* reports, funded by the Annie E. Casey Foundation. County, state, and national *Kids Count Data* are available in hard copy for student use in our Educational Media Center. Data are also available on the South Carolina Kids Count WEB page. In addition, students are encouraged to use their personal observations during the first few weeks of class. Instructions and opportunities to practice several observational techniques often utilized in the study of child development are part of the first five weeks of structured field experience. As students practice using their newly acquired observation skills, their personal observations may help them identify areas of need. As another method of need identification, students are encouraged to interview teachers and the principal of the school where they are observing to discover needs which may have been identified and prioritized through planning activities at the school. Finally, young middle school students who have been involved with service learning are invited to present descriptions of their service learning experiences to the classes, including a description of the needs they addressed. In addition to seeing the need identification process modeled by middle school students, pre-service teachers have a first-hand opportunity to view the personal development of middle school students that results from service learning.

After identifying the need they wish to address, students develop a written plan either individually or as part of a team. Following approval, the students implement the plan and then reflect on the results in writing. At the end of the semester, students briefly give an oral presentation of their service learning experience and their personal reflection as part of a class celebration. Among the needs that have been addressed by students are those related to early literacy, nutritional practices, hygiene, math skills development, homework, special needs for individual children, and parenting information.

Level Three

Other examples of connecting pre-service teachers with real life experiences occur during the junior year in various methods courses. In the *Early Childhood Education Program*, the focus is on improving the pre-service teachers' ability to work with parents, especially in Kindergarten and First Grade. Students design and produce learning bags to support parent and child interaction. A proposal was submitted and funded to support the connection between the college classroom and the public preschool program.

In the *Elementary Science Methods* class, students are given extra credit for teaching a needed science lesson in the community. In the *Elementary Mathematics Methods* class, students are required to identify a need and to formulate and implement a plan to address that need. Examples have included tutoring and developing individualized lessons and teaching materials for students experiencing difficulty in particular mathematics content areas like fractions, multiplication tables, whole number division and pre-algebra concepts. Students report on their service learning through personal reactions and written reflections.

Pre-service teachers in the *Language Arts Methods* class correspond with eighth graders via e-mail throughout the semester. They provide service in the following ways: an audience for young writers; insight and information about college life; and information about making career choices. In the Secondary English Methods class, students are creating a museum exhibit at the Pickens County Museum commemorating Ben Robertson's *Red Hills and Cotton, An Upcountry Memoir*. Ben Robertson was a WWII correspondent, a friend of Edward R. Murrow, and a Clemson University graduate. The pre-service teachers are learning to educate high school students and the public through an interactive exhibit using multi-media applications.

Level Four

South Carolina has recently adopted the ADEPT (Assisting, Developing, and Evaluating Professional Teaching) Model for teacher assessment. Students in the Teacher Education program at Clemson University are evaluated during their student teacher experience using this model. Although the service learning method incorporates most of the ADEPT Dimensions, service learning particularly strengthens pre-service and in-service teachers' skills and abilities for addressing the following dimensions: Long-Range Planning; Short-Range Planning; High Expectations; Instructional Strategies; and Beyond the Classroom.

Two faculty members in Special Education, through the South Carolina Center of Excellence in Rural Special Education, provided opportunities for student teachers to design and implement a service learning project at the school in which they were student teaching. The Center of Excellence provided a small grant to support their project. All students, on behalf of the schools in which they were teaching, wrote and submitted proposals to support service learning. Several of the proposals were funded and have provided opportunities for other students to participate in activities.

The Vision

Our vision for teacher education at Clemson University is a more coordinated, systemic approach to the integration of service learning throughout the Teacher Education Program. Service learning is not a panacea, but an effective method for connecting classroom knowledge with real life applications. Service learning is a natural vehicle for addressing the School-to-Work initiative. Ultimately, we envision that every student, at graduation, will have had a number of well-placed, well-designed service learning experiences which have been mentored by well-informed and experienced faculty who utilize technological tools as appropriate. The focus will remain on the quality of experiences, rather than on a number of required clock hours. We envision a journey, not a destination.

In support of the journey, we have begun work in two areas. Students and faculty are creating an electronic and hard copy publication that will provide a forum for conversation, discussion, and reflections regarding the practice of service learning as a teaching methodology. This effort is supported through a small South Carolina Association of Teacher Educators SCATE grant and will continue to expand as additional funding is obtained. Thus far, the proposed publication has connected Clemson University students and faculty in a common goal. The vision is that the publication will connect Clemson University

Teacher Education students and faculty with Public School students and faculty. The second area focuses on strengthening the assessment of service learning experiences of students, teachers, and community partners. We are presently field testing three assessment tools designed to measure the impact of service learning.

Reflection 1: A Developing Practice

I've always felt a need to have students connect classroom learning to real life activities. Mathematics has traditionally been taught as an abstract subject, and the need to make it more applied at the elementary level is a necessity as well as a challenge.

Before I became aware of the term service learning, and certainly the methodology, I searched for opportunities to have my methods students experience the connection between theory and practice. As early as 1992, an opportunity presented itself that afforded my students the chance to develop and present mathematical activities to children in grades 1-5 in a local elementary school. Students were paired and assigned to a particular grade level. We were exploring the use of manipulatives in our classroom, so a natural application was to take these materials and develop activities and games that would teach or reinforce a mathematical concept or skill. This was a very successful endeavor. Students learned the value of planning and the necessity for being flexible. Students had very positive reactions and were challenged by the effort and energy that was necessary to implement activities that held the attention of the children and addressed the cognitive aspects of learning.

As with any project, this one had barriers or obstacles. Scheduling was problematic. The public school needed the students from 2:00 until 2:45 p.m. The university classes in which the students were enrolled met from 11:00 until 1:45 (2 sections), therefore, creative juggling of university schedules and classroom participation was necessary to accommodate the needs of the public school. Transportation was a problem for some students. In some cases, schedules and assignments of grade levels had to be changed to accommodate car pools.

Working to overcome the barriers was worth the effort. Reflective conversations and reports showed a real connection with the children. Students were surprised that the need to maintain discipline was so great. They were challenged by the range of levels within a class, but they were overwhelmed by the devotion, dedication, and respect shown them by the children. Many of them equated it to a religious experience and said that their decision to teach was solidified.

My present adaptation of service learning methodology builds on my previous experience. I do not attempt to schedule or coordinate transportation arrangements. The service learning component is a part of the course, not an optional add-on. Students are required to search the local community and determine a need that can be addressed through their mathematical expertise. They are encouraged to contact day-care centers, after school programs, homework centers, churches, and local schools. There has been no shortage of opportunities. Some students were already tutoring on a one-on-one basis, and just needed to be more reflective in their actions. Some students found opportunities in their home towns during holiday periods and made significant contributions. Most of the students volunteered in local after school and tutoring programs. All of the students had glowing reports regarding their contributions. They felt they really made a difference. They were required to spend five (5) hours, but most continued to go back because they had developed personal relationships with the children.

Reflection 2: A Professional Journey

The specific experience which introduced me to service learning, as a methodology, was the development of a proposal submitted to the South Carolina State Department of Education to fund a Service Learning Institute for twenty-five classroom teachers in upstate South Carolina. When the proposal was funded, I developed a detailed bibliography of service learning publications and materials, began ordering them, and started reading. What eventually, although not immediately, became clear to me was that service learning enables me, as a faculty member, to simultaneously address the three-pronged mission of our land-grant university: teaching, research, and service while working on my professional agenda, which is to improve the lives of children and their families. Part of my agenda is to develop the capacity within pre-service teachers to identify needs which impact teaching and learning. A second part of my agenda is to develop the skills of pre-service teachers to work collaboratively within their communities to improve the lives of children and families.

Including all students more equitably in our educational system began to emerge from my early professional experiences as an important need. Experiences with two students during my student teaching days created a long-lasting impact, which contributed to the establishment of my professional agenda. Likewise, students at a Vocational Technical School who were studying *Child Care* taught me that our educational system misses the mark with many potentially good students. Therefore, bringing students who were on the fringes of learning into the mainstream of my classes has been an important goal from the beginning of my teaching career. I have searched continuously for ways to do it, always learning from the experiences of trying, but not always succeeding in meeting the goal.

My first experiences with students whose potential was marred through drug use, at least when I was knowledgeable enough to recognize and understand some of the signals, occurred while in graduate school. Briefly, I tutored in a program designed to assist students in getting their General Education Development certificate (GED). I watched as the motivation for education was overwhelmed by the desire or need for drugs. Usual discipline approaches did not work. As a teacher, I was frustrated. I felt unskilled in how to harvest the potential in students who were coping with drug addiction. I sought knowledge and answers. I became involved as a volunteer in a local agency and learned much through that experience about the early efforts of prevention which focused, in that program, on improving family communication. The program was effective in teaching the concepts of the program, however, it did not reach into many families and communities where the needs were greatest.

During graduate school, my husband who is a professional in a similar area, invited me to team with him to use what we had learned and experienced to design and implement two parts of a national impact study for a youth organization. We approached the evaluation from a prevention and developmental point of view, a different approach from the traditional understanding of that organization's impact. Reviewing the literature and using our own experiences, we conceptualized a model and developed two national documents. Although the same work that guided us was also the foundation for service learning, we did not make that connection until later.

We have both been dedicated to positive development of all children and youth, regardless of socioeconomic level, or any other potential risk

factor. The model we developed has guided our work for many years.
My husband dubbed it the 3 C's, in part for the simplicity of the name,
however each "C" represents one of three comprehensive and complex
components identified through research literature review. We believe
that if children's needs are met and they develop competency, coping,
and contributory skills, their outcomes will be positive. Early pioneers
of service learning, researchers Hedin and Conrad, influenced the
development of the 3 C's model. The goals I establish for my
professional service and research and much of my teaching are
consistent with this model. My goals are all related to removing
barriers and developing capacity for positive human development. I am
constantly seeking to improve my understanding and practice in regard
to this model.

During my early years of teaching at Clemson University, I became
aware that many of our students made comments that revealed a dislike
for students they might one day teach. I was deeply concerned and
wanted to change the situation. At about the same time, a colleague
who was teaching one section of Child Growth and Development,
shared two questions she had asked the students and the results. She
asked them how many of them came from intact, nuclear families and
how many had grandparents who had graduated from college? The
percentage of students from nuclear families was about 90%,
astonishingly high for 1989. As a first generation college graduate, I
thought the percentage of students with grandparents who had
graduated from college would be around 5%, however, it was higher,
closer to 30%. My colleague and I wondered aloud if this could be a
fluke. During the next ten years, I have asked the question in every
section of the Child Growth and Development course that I have taught.
The figures do vary, but they were not a fluke. The percentage of
intact, nuclear families is always above 80%, most often around 90%.
The percentage of students with grandparents who graduated from
college has fluctuated slightly more, between 20% and 50%. These
figures have not been formally collected, but have been systematically
noted, nonetheless. As I thought about this, it became very clear that
our pre-service teacher education students are very different from the
students they will one day teach. Then I began to understand why they
might express dislike for some of their future students -- they were
different! I began to work on ways to increase their tolerance. I tried
exhortation, testing, strategic field placements. None of these methods

worked as well as I wanted them to work. Then came the service learning proposal!

The more I have learned about service learning and the research on which it is based, the more I believe in its effectiveness for changing attitudes. During 1996-97, I implemented a service learning component in all four sections of *Child Growth and Development* and in the single section of *The Behavior of the Preschool Child,* which I taught. As part of the preparation for service learning, all students in *Child Growth and Development* were required to participate in a group initiatives experience at the Clemson University Outdoor Laboratory. In addition, middle school service learning ambassadors were invited into all the classes to teach students the method of service learning. Assistance was provided for any student or group of students, as needed, throughout the planning stages. Students were required to identify a need related to children 0-12 years, which they addressed through service learning. They reflected on their learning and celebrated by sharing their experiences and being recognized for their contributions. The student's reflection papers revealed powerful changes in terms of personal and professional knowledge gain, understandings, applications, and judgments. Student comments regarding service learning on evaluations were positive. When I read the 80 reflection papers each semester, I am deeply moved by the power of their learning. In fact, I am systematically studying the impact of service learning on the personal and professional development of pre-service teacher education students.

In 1997-98, I continued to refine the service learning methodology for *Child Growth and Development.* I utilized e-mail for communication and teaching, worked to improve the planning processes used by students, worked to improve the presentations of service learning projects given by students, and worked to develop innovative ways to integrate assessment of service learning into regular class exams. One assessment method used a service learning opportunity to assess students' ability to apply material in the text to a real community need.

Students in *Child Development* used information about early literacy to create a page for the Greenville ChildWatch 1998 notebook. Master's students in an *Early Literacy* class critiqued the *Child Development* students' first drafts which were returned to the students for revisions. Students revised their draft and submitted them for final grading. Their score counted as 26% of their third exam. In addition, I introduced a final exam critical incident assessment of their service learning experience.

During these four semesters, and through this service learning effort, I have linked student resources (approximately 80 students each semester) to various sites through service learning projects, which provided a wide range of services to children 0-12 years of age. In addition, during both of these years, I have worked to establish a unique partnership with an after school program in a predominately African-American community setting. As part of that partnership, students have been placed at the site for both field experience and approved service learning experiences. The part of this partnership which pleases me most is that a former *Child Growth and Development* student who first worked at the after school program as part of her service learning project is now directing the program and providing supervision for current student placements. The partnership with the after school program has worked well. Of the students involved, several made deep commitments to the children. Through their participation, they gained experience that they indicated taught them how to handle challenging behavior. They also indicated a new confidence level in doing so. My personal experience at the site, when I have participated by speaking and then listening throughout an entire Saturday afternoon program for parents and when I have tutored one afternoon a week, has been hugely rewarding and instructive. I have also learned from this experience that placing students in a different cultural setting does not ensure cultural understanding. For some students, cultural stereotypes were reinforced. When I challenged these stereotypes, some students were not pleased. I am still working on how to create change in this area. I suspect there will not be an easy, painless way to do it. Partly as a result of this experience, I coordinated the application of three faculty members for diversity facilitator training through the National Corporation of Service.

During these two years, I have worked to share service learning with my colleagues by involving them in small grant applications and by making presentations to classes. Several have used service learning with at least one class, some have provided a service learning experience for all special education student teachers because of its effectiveness in overcoming social and other barriers for special education students.

The next area that I plan to strengthen is the use of technology (especially my WEB page) to facilitate service learning. Several students have given permission for their work to be used as models on the WEB page or in a notebook of examples of student plans and reflections.

There have been so many examples of how service learning has strengthened my own teaching and enriched the learning experiences for students. In one instance, I shared my area of expertise and my personal collection and bibliography of children's books related to service learning with a doctoral student, who spent approximately 15 hours reading additional children's books and selecting titles for me to review. I read the books she suggested and made final selections to add to the bibliography. The next year, we both spent two full days reading children's books to complete a Bibliography of Children's Literature Related to service learning. During this process, the doctoral student taught a high school student, who assisted us, to annotate. (I had previously taught the same student to use APA style and to build a bibliography. The young student worked with me to develop a detailed bibliography on service learning, which the National Dropout Prevention Center has distributed freely and anonymously). We, all three, participated in a regional conference wherein we presented our original work. A much revised version of this work will be published next year as a monograph through the South Carolina Office of National Service.

During 1996-97, I worked with a student long-distance in a *Seminar in Human Growth and Development*, a master's level course. I challenged her to use her Spanish-speaking skills to work with a group of preschool children as a self-directed adult learning project. She was to apply what she knew about language development to the development of the Spanish curriculum. She did, and this may be the only example in South Carolina of teaching a foreign language to preschool children in a day care setting.

Most recently, as a researcher for the *Call Me Mister* project, I have a wonderful opportunity to incorporate service learning into the support curricula for the participants in the project. This project is designed to place 200 African American male teachers in elementary classrooms during the next 5 years.

Service learning permeates my professional life. It has been the focus of publications, presentations, curricula design, PTAR guidelines, professional collaborations, funding proposals, and much, much more. Service learning has empowered me to teach, to inquire, to learn, and to serve. In the words of my professional agenda, service learning has improved my capacity to develop the three C's: competency, coping, and contributing skills.

Chapter Ten

Technical Writing

Barbara E. Weaver

Abstract

Using service learning is a highly effective way to teach the course content of technical writing. The main objective is to provide a meaningful way for students to analyze an audience, perform research, practice using standard communication formats, and work on a team to serve a client. The students select their teams and clients based on their interests and propose the creation of a communication deliverable to meet their client's needs. Examples of the deliverables are brochures, Web sites, published articles, and public service announcements. The outcome is significant growth personally, intellectually, and socially for students and a better community for us all.

The Class

At Clemson University, technical writing is part of the general education requirements for students in technical majors, such as engineering, architecture, construction science management, agriculture, nursing, pre-medicine, mathematics, and science. Occasionally I have a student majoring in English or graphic communication. Students must be at least juniors to register for the course; most of my students are seniors. Typically students put off taking the course because they fear it will be horribly boring with a focus on grammar, spelling and, from their perspective, meaningless textbook assignments.

Historical Review

The first day of class, my students are surprised to learn that they are required to undertake an authentic project for a university or community organization. I began using authentic projects spring semester 1997, when my two sections of technical writing worked on complex and demanding projects for BMW Manufacturing Corporation in Greer, South Carolina, and IBM Corporation in Austin, Texas. Our primary contacts at BMW and IBM were members of the Pearce Center for Professional Communication Corporate Advisory Board. As a member of the Pearce Center's Research Team, I was willing to experiment with these projects; I wanted to enhance the coursework and give my students opportunities to learn outside the classroom. That semester changed the way I would teach forever.

The BMW project involved auditing the Greer plant's communication practices, evaluating those practices, and recommending ways to improve communication. Teams of students examined the plant's newsletter, shift reports, personnel handbook, and other pertinent plant documents; met with various employees for one-on-one interviews; and observed meetings at all levels, of every division, and all shifts of the organization. The time of the meetings coupled with the travel time (over an hour one way) meant that some students didn't get back to campus until well after midnight and other students had to leave campus at 3:00 a.m. The multiple trips (six in two weeks) and the arranging of transportation was daunting.

The IBM project involved developing a plan, budget, and schedule for migrating documentation of an IBM product to a new development tool, installing new hardware and software for each writer assigned to the product, training writers to use the new hardware and software platform, and meeting the release dates of the product. Student teams communicated frequently with IBM employees through e-mail and, on one occasion, by video conferencing. The tools of communication were a tremendous help, but the intricacies of IBM accounting and the IBM lexicon were not things we could master in six weeks.

The BMW and IBM projects were good projects, but for many reasons they were inappropriate for my students. The most important reason was that the projects drove the course content and kept us from reaching my course objectives and goals. The students learned a lot about the two corporations, meeting deadlines, and working in teams. But only a few gained experience in writing the final reports, developing the electronic presentations, and delivering the presentations at the Pearce Center's Corporate Advisory Board meeting. The projects were better suited for a small graduate seminar in professional communication. But we did see positive results from the projects: several students received job offers during interviews when they showed the recruiters their final reports and the program from the board meeting.

As the end of the semester neared, I realized that I was on the brink of something powerful: service learning would provide all the positive aspects and reduce, if not eliminate, all of the negative aspects of the BMW and IBM projects. Small businesses close to campus, university organizations, not-for-profit organizations, and the community service arms of corporations would be equipped to work with people from a wide range of disciplines and would appreciate the student help because otherwise the work might not get done. The students would benefit by seeing their results make a positive difference in the community. That summer I began using service learning to teach course content and each semester since then has been better than the last.

Preparation and Action

Because of my experience with the BMW and IBM projects, I am extremely careful about project selection. My technical writing course objectives are for students to: analyze an audience; research the issues; write a proposal; write status reports; write meeting minutes; use e-mail; work on a team; work with a client; write a project plan and schedule; make an oral presentation to the community; design and develop a deliverable; and write a final report.

Those objectives involve skills that students in technical majors need to know how to do. One of the important lessons I learned from the

BMW and IBM projects is that students perform better when they have a choice. I now leave the project development to my students, and I with their chosen clients approve or disapprove their project proposals. When considering their proposals, I first check to make sure the project will allow the course objectives to be met. Then I evaluate the project to make sure undergraduates can successfully complete the project in six weeks. If the project meets those requirements, I look at their projected budgets and funding, as well as electronic equipment needs and delegation of duties. While the projects must be challenging, I try to set up my students for success rather than allow them to take on an inappropriate project that may frustrate instead of enhance their learning experience.

When we begin the service learning portion of the semester, I sometimes present basic information about organizations and their potential projects; other times potential clients come to class to present their needs directly to the students. Occasionally students know of an organization in need of help or are concerned about a particular social issue and request my permission to pursue that option.

For example, spring semester 1998 one of my students was especially concerned about date rape. She solicited other students to work with her to create more community awareness about the problem and what victims should do in the case of rape. The team worked closely with the City of Clemson victim's advocate, the Pickens County court system, and Sandy Woodward (a local communication and marketing consultant). They even solicited help from friends outside the class to generate awareness of the problem. The team published an article in the student publication, *The Tiger*, created and distributed flyers that provided current rape statistics in the area and what victims should do, wrote and produced a public service announcement that still airs on two local radio stations, and developed and delivered a truly powerful electronic presentation that clearly captured the attention of the community audience.

Clients who are willing to come to class to explain their organization's needs often generate more interest than I can. For example, spring semester 1998 Professor Frances Chamberlain, from Clemson's landscape architecture department, told my students about her collaborative project with the South Carolina Botanical Garden. She explained that two French artists were coming to Clemson University February 1 and in just 28 days they would locate a site and then design and install, with the help of her studio students, the fifth

land sculpture in the Botanical Garden. Professor Chamberlain's
enthusiasm was infectious.

Five teams of students formed to help promote the land sculpture
project. The student teams wrote proposals to provide Professor
Chamberlain with the following documentation: an article for the
College of Architecture, Arts and Humanities publication, *Mirare*; an
article for the *South Carolina Botanical Garden Quarterly*; a biography
of the two artists for the architecture library; a four-color brochure with
a short description of each land sculpture and a map showing how to
find each sculpture in the garden; and an article for the publication, *The
Tiger*.

As I mentioned earlier, students formed their teams based on their
interests. I encourage students to form teams of three. Typically teams
of more than three have a difficult time dividing the work equally and
find that scheduling meetings that all members can attend is almost
impossible. Teams of less than three often find the project too difficult
to complete in the time we have – only six weeks from the day they
hear about the various possibilities to the day their final reports are due
to the clients.

The students working on the Botanical Garden projects began their
research by joining Professor Chamberlain's studio students at a dinner
for the artists, Marc Babarit and Gilles Bruni, held at Professor
Chamberlain's home. That initial experience set the tone for the entire
project. The students reported that they had never been invited to a
faculty member's home before. By opening her home to my students,
Professor Chamberlain created an environment of inclusion. My
students understood that Professor Chamberlain expected them to make
a positive difference in the success of the land sculpture project.

The students continued their research by attending lectures given by
Babarit and Bruni, attending Professor Chamberlain's studio class, and
helping install "The Stream Path." They documented the project by
keeping observational notes, taking photographs, and interviewing
Babarit, Bruni, and other students involved with the land sculpture.
The highlight for one student was his research facilitated by Professor
John Bednar, from Clemson's languages department. Professor Bednar
hosted my student at a private dinner with Babarit and Bruni and served
as interpreter so my student could get more in-depth answers to his
technical questions. Professor Bednar also translated documents only

available in French to help my student gain a better understanding of the artists' philosophy and previous work.

Weekly oral status reports presented in class gave the students a chance to compare notes, discuss difficulties they faced, and discover viable solutions. The status report must answer three questions: What has your team accomplished in the past week? What does your team plan to accomplish in the coming week? What roadblocks does your team face and how might those roadblocks affect your schedule? Those three questions provide the framework students need to select information to include in a status report.   Because the status reports are delivered orally to the class, the students get practice speaking to a group. What I like best about the oral status reports is that they can lead to healthy class discussion, wider collaboration, and creative problem solving. For example, I require each team to develop and deliver, to a community audience, an electronic presentation about their project results. In one status report, the team expressed a need for a close-up picture of Babarit and Bruni for their presentation. Even in all the rolls of film my students had used, no one in the class had a good, close-up photograph of the artists. By brainstorming solutions, the students decided they should check with Ernie Denny, director of cultural programs at the Botanical Garden. The next week the team reported that Mr. Denny did not have a close up photo either, but he did have a good quality photograph of the artists they could manipulate in PhotoShop to achieve the effect they wanted.

My class meets in a lab with state-of-the-art computer equipment and software, including scanners, a digital camera, multimedia projection, voice recording equipment, video duplication and digitizing equipment, sound clips, clip art, MS Office, Adobe PageMaker, Adobe PhotoShop, and more. The students learn to use the equipment and software that they need to meet their client's needs. Usually students use everything in the lab except the video equipment, which has only been used by a few students.   Because the students need to learn the computer technology to please their clients, they are anxious to learn and waste no time. When they need to know how to do something that I don't know how to do, they put their heads together to figure it out, we call an expert to help, or they fall back on a contingency plan.

Reflection and Celebration

When developing their electronic presentations for the community audience, the students have an opportunity to reflect on what they've accomplished. I require them to include the following: a description of their client's organization, its purpose and mission; an explanation of the organization's need; a thorough explanation of the team's project, how the team envisioned the project meeting the organization's need, what the team members did, what the results are, and how well those results meet the organization's need; recommendations for the client's use of the team's deliverable and any other recommendations that could help the client with future plans; a description of what the team members learned from the project; and a thank you to the client and any other people who helped the team members achieve their goals.

The presentation requirements demand that the students spend quality time reflecting on their projects, the community, and themselves. The audience for the students' presentations is their classmates, students from other classes, invited guests from on and off campus (college deans and other administrators from on campus, the mayor and other city officials from off campus), and their clients. While the students are initially nervous about presenting to a large group of people, they soon learn that they are the experts on their projects and that they can address any question anyone may ask. I am convinced that because they know they have to present to this community audience they are more motivated to perform at a high level. By the night of the presentations, they are well rehearsed and ready to favorablyimpress everyone in attendance. No team has ever failed to rise to the occasion. Their successful presentations provide an opportunity for the students to receive recognition for their contributions to their community. Refreshments served the evening of the presentations give the event a sense of celebration.

Another opportunity I began offering my students with the BMW and IBM
projects is to discuss their projects on the WAHT 1560 AM *Golden Corner Radio Magazine*, an hour-long live show that focuses on community issues. Students volunteer to be interviewed by the show's host; they are not given questions beforehand, so they must think quickly on their feet. If the students bring an audiocassette tape, WAHT tapes the show and then makes copies for the students.

We also have a post-project review after the final reports are completed and a full project folder with the deliverable has been given to the client. Usually we celebrate the project completion at my house. For example, spring semester 1998 I fixed dinner for the 50 students and they brought desserts, drinks and ice. During the informal portion of the celebration, we played the radio show tape; the students who were not able to attend because they were in another class or some other activity they couldn't miss enjoyed hearing what their classmates had to say.

During the formal part of our celebration, we discussed three things: What went right? What went wrong? What can be done in the future to make the service projects better for students and the community? The information the students provide at these post-project reviews has been tremendously helpful to me as I plan for the next semester.

The academic and work experience portfolios my students create and the final exam also provide the students a chance to reflect. As they select coursework from all their academic work at Clemson, develop new materials to demonstrate the skills they've learned from various jobs, and add their service project materials, they invariably begin to see how they have developed into talented, thoughtful people with valuable skills they can market. Frequently, they will have thank you letters or notes of praise from their clients and others that saw their presentations. Those words of praise and thanks from others are important to the students and are always included in their portfolios. For the final exam, I ask them to write a two-page essay that discusses the effects of all the course assignments on them personally, intellectually, and socially. By that time, they have developed significant confidence in who they are, what they want and need from life, and what they can give back to potential employers and their community.

The Projects

The projects and the resulting deliverables depend on the students' interests and their clients' needs. During the Spring semester 1998, the deliverables my 50 students created were:

➤ Various publications to promote the nature-based sculptures in the South Carolina Botanical Garden.

➤ A news article, flyers, and radio public service announcement to increase community awareness of rape.

➤ A four-color brochure to help with recruitment for Clemson University Women's Basketball.

➤ A brochure that explains available help for student-athletes with learning disabilities for Clemson University's Student-Athlete Enrichment Program.

➤ An informational brochure for the Clemson University student chapter of Habitat for Humanity.

➤ A Web site for the Women in Agriculture sorority on campus.

➤ A Web site for Clemson University's Disabilities Services office.

➤ A Web site for the new biomedical major at Clemson University.

➤ A Web site for WAHT 1560 AM, a local radio station that focuses on community service.

➤ A four-color brochure on the ceramic engineering major at Clemson University.

➤ A promotional brochure for the new Triathlon Club on campus.

➤ A front and back flyer created from six current documents to reduce inventory problems and printing costs for Fike Recreation Center on campus.

➤ An article explaining the differences between rebuilding and restoring a historical building, as evidenced by the rebuilding of Calhoun Corners, a restaurant which had been housed in one of Clemson's oldest buildings until it burned to the ground October 31, 1997.

➤ A new logo and an information card intended for victims of domestic violence for WORTHouse, Clemson's shelter for battered women.

Each project required the students to analyze multiple audiences, work closely with their teammates and their clients, thoroughly research their topics, use various formats for communication, and learn to use computer hardware and software they had not used before. Some of the projects required that students deal with legal issues, such as copyright, trademark, and registered trademark permissions.

Through the oral status reports, all the students gained exposure to the legal issues even if they did not face those issues directly. In just six weeks the students acquired significant skills they will need in their technical careers and made contributions to their community.

Evaluations

   Grading team projects is especially difficult. When students are involved in community service projects, they sometimes have a hard time understanding how and when they will be graded. As the teacher, I appreciate that student perspective and make my expectations clear. Equally important is for students to understand that they are not just working for a grade. They have others outside the classroom that are counting on them to perform well and make a difference in the community. To help my students understand how they will be graded, I provide them with a checklist, which is shown in Figure 1.

Figure 1. Project Checklist

The Deliverable for Your Client

_____ The deliverable is grammatically and mechanically error-free.

_____ The deliverable demonstrates that the team members are skilled writers, who are aware of the audience and purpose of the deliverable.

_____ The deliverable meets or exceeds the expectations of the client.

_____ The final report (with appropriate materials referenced in the report attached) has been given to the client.

_____ The deliverable has been given to the client. In many cases, the deliverable should be given to the client in both electronic and printed versions.

The Project Package for Your Teacher

_____ All the documents in the package are grammatically and mechanically error-free.

_____ All the documents in combination show a clear picture of the project from beginning to end.

_____ All the documents demonstrate that the team members are skilled writers, who are aware of the audience and purpose for each document.

_____ The documents are organized in a logical order.

_____ The final report (with appropriate materials referenced in the report attached) is included.

_____ The signed proposal is included.

_____ The plan and schedule are included.

_____ The PowerPoint status report slides (printed on paper) are included.

_____ The minutes for all meetings are included.

_____ The PowerPoint community presentation slides (printed on paper) are included.

_____ The deliverable is included, in the case of Web pages, the URL is provided.

To determine the client's level of satisfaction and to ensure that the students have given their client everything they are supposed to, I ask the clients for their evaluation of the student teams. Figure 2 is the form I send to the clients.

Figure 2. Team Evaluation Form

Student Names: (I fill in the appropriate names.)
Project: (I fill in the appropriate project title.)
Please place an "x" beside your answer.

Did the students give you an opportunity to review their work before they finalized it?
yes _____ no _____

If yes, how well did they address your review comments in their revision?
outstanding _____ good _____ average _____ poor _____ not at all _____

If no, how much of a negative effect did their failure to ask for your review have on the final product?
none _____ little _____ some _____ significant _____ detrimental _____

How pleased are you with the final product the students created?
delighted _____ very satisfied _____ adequately satisfied _____
barely satisfied _____ not at all satisfied _____

Have the students given you the final product?
electronically? _____ printed? _____ other? _____

Have the students given you a final report on the project?
yes   _____   no   _____

Did the students work with you in a professional manner (punctual for scheduled meetings, effective and appropriate communication with you, etc.)?
yes   _____   no   _____

If no, please state below specifically how they failed to act professionally.

Is there anything else the students told you they would provide you that they haven't yet given you?
yes   _____   no   _____

If yes, please note below what they still owe you.

What else should I know about this student team?

Spring semester 1998, only one team failed to get the highest rating to every question I asked the clients. Along with the completed form, many of the clients sent me their thanks for working with the students to serve the community.

Challenges and Benefits

Using service learning in technical writing is challenging, especially the demands on my time. With two sections of 25 students each, I usually have 16 projects to manage. The meeting minutes are a big help in keeping track of who is doing what. I require the students to rotate the responsibility of writing the minutes and e-mailing them to me. The minutes must include the following:

1. The project title
2. The date and location of the meeting
3. Who attended the meeting
4. A summary of the discussion and any decisions that were made
5. Action items including who is assigned the action and when the action is to be completed

If I notice that a student does not regularly attend meetings, a student does not appear to be accepting action items, or a student seems to be accepting more than a fair share of the action items, I can discuss my observation with the team and guide the students into a more balanced distribution of work. The meeting minutes and the status reports keep me abreast of each team's progress without too much additional work.

Another concern when sending students into the community is student behavior. I have never experienced any inappropriate behavior by my students, but to help them understand the importance of this issue, we spend one class period going over appropriate behavior when they represent the class, faculty, and university in the community. One of the most important rules is client confidentiality. When working on the BMW projects, we had to sign a non-disclosure agreement; however, all clients deserve the same loyalty even if no agreement is signed. Students are cautioned not to discuss client business unless they have permission from the client.

Money is a problem, but not insurmountable. Spring semester 1998, a mini-grant from Clemson University's Service Learning Collaborative helped pay for printing of the client deliverables. In addition to those funds, students solicited in-kind donations from a local print shop, and the students and I contributed financially. Because the projects were for worthy organizations with limited funding of their own, the students and I saw our financial contributions to the projects as part of our community service.

No matter how difficult the challenges may be, I always have lots of energy when my students are working on their service projects. The reason for that energy is the significant growth I see in my students. The best description of their growth comes in their own words:

Every time I go into Fike, I'm going to see this brochure and know that I did it. And it will be the best one there!

They trusted us enough to tell us where WORTHouse is. (The location of the battered women's shelter is highly protected information.)

I know now that I can make an oral presentation to an audience of three-piece business suits.

I didn't realize in the midst of the project that I was learning anything. But once the project was over, I realized that I had learned a great deal about writing, oral communication, design, audience, teamwork, research, how to work with a client, and lots of computer technology I never expected to use in an English class. I even learned a lot about the South Carolina Botanical Garden and art.

Coming into this class, I was expecting to write letters, resumes, and business memos. Never did I think that I would be as challenged as I was from the first day.

This class gave me a sense of self worth that I have not had since high school.

Summary and Conclusion

Using service learning in technical writing is the best way I know to teach course content. The students reap benefits far beyond my early expectations. Frequently previous students call me, stop by my office, or catch me while walking across campus to tell me they have landed a job because of the skills they learned through their service project. One of my students, who now works in sports marketing, recently told me, "I had to do a brochure for a project last week, and the only reason I knew how to do it was your class."

One student comment that always makes me smile just to remember it came from an architecture student who worked on the Botanical Garden project: "I never thought it would be an English class that put me in a garden where I got my hands and feet muddy." What that student didn't realize was that a short time ago I, too, would have had trouble visualizing a writing assignment that would demand my students to slosh around in a muddy garden during the cold and rainy days of February 1998. Now, I can't imagine anything less. I expect my students to jump in with both feet and get their hands dirty with meaningful, authentic projects.

INDEX

horticulture; planning and landscape architecture; and
    sociology, 29
organizational communication, 76
Rutgers University, 3
Sample Contract, 83-84
Science, 7, 99
Senior Service Corps, 25
Service Learning Collaborative, Clemson University, 5, 20, 25, 101,
    102
Service Learning Framework, 5
    preparation, 5, 11, 40, 52, 61, 104, 128, 141
    action, 5, 11, 12, 41, 52, 61, 104, 106, 128, 141
    reflection, 5, 11, 12, 24, 26, 44, 54, 62, 94, 104, 109, 128,
    131, 132, 145
    celebration/recognition, 5,11, 13, 26, 45, 54, 62, 94, 104, 110,
    128, 145
Skills of Life Chart, 96
Sociology, 6, 23
South Carolina Association of Teacher Educators (SCATE), 130
South Carolina Botanical Garden, 142
South Carolina Commission on Higher Education, 100
South Carolina Kids Count, 128
South Carolina State Department of Education, 132
Southern Regional Educational Board, 1
"Sprouting Wings Program", 25
Teacher Education, 7
Team Evaluation Form, 150
Technical Writing, 7, 139
Tenets of Clemson University Service Learning, 97-98
University for Action (UYA), 1
WORTHouse, 152

Biographical Sketch of Authors:

An Orientation to Service Learning

Marty Duckenfield is Public Information Director for the National Dropout Prevention Center at Clemson University and has coordinated the Clemson University Service Learning Collaborative since 1996. She received her BA from Bates College and her M.N.S. from Clemson University. Her extensive experience in service learning can be seem in some of her former and current activities which include: teaching a Masters level service learning course; development of numerous service learning resources; facilitating dozens of workshops at state, regional, and national conferences. Additionally, she has represented the NDPC since 1993 in various capacities including most recently the regional information center for the South in the new Learn and Serve national Service Learning Clearinghouse.

Steven J. Madden (see "Organizational Communication").

Psychology

Patricia A. Connor-Greene is Alumni Distinguished Professor of Psychology at Clemson University. She received her BA from Wells College in 1976 and her Ph.D. in Clinical/Community Psychology from the University of South Carolina in 1983. She has incorporated service learning projects into courses in Abnormal Psychology, Psychology and Culture, and Women and Psychology.

Horticulture; Planning and Landscape Architecture; and Sociology

Mary Taylor Haque, ASLA, RLA,   is a landscape architect and Professor in the Department of Horticulture at Clemson University whose expertise is teaching and design. She has made community outreach an integral part of her teaching and scholarship for twenty years. She has taught 15 different courses and is dedicated to creating an active learning environment, engaging and empowering her students. She has designed or supervised designs for over 164 projects across the state of South Carolina and internationally, and is dedicated to instilling an ethic of community service into her students.   Projects include residences, hospitals, schools, industrial parks and even whole cities. Students visit sites, consult with homeowners, company presidents, school boards, mayors, city councils, etc. as they work through a well planned process including research, analysis, conceptual plans, preliminary plans, and final project presentations.

Lolly Tai, ASLA, RLA, is a landscape architect and a professor whose philosophy is to design with an environmentally sensitive approach. She believes in the importance of being responsible stewards and designing with the land as opposed to against the land. Her private practice is characterized by projects with a diversity of scope and scale ranging from residential estate, commercial, resort, community planning, recreational facility, botanical garden and xeriscape designs. Her work has been recognized through design awards, publications, exhibits and presentations at national, regional and local levels. Tai who received her masters degree from Harvard University and bachelors degree from Cornell University has enriched her career with projects where design is essential.   She is a registered landscape architect in Connecticut, New Jersey, New York, North Carolina and South Carolina. She currently serves as the president of the South Carolina American Society of Landscape Architects, vice-chair of the South Carolina Landscape Architecture Advisory Council and a member of the Council of Educators in Landscape Architecture.

Brenda Vander Mey, Ph.D., is Associate Professor of Sociology and Coordinator, South Carolina Landscapes for Learning collaborative. She and her students have been involved in service-learning for over a decade. In addition, Dr. Vander Mey has been involved in participatory learning landscape activities in her community for many years, and recently has expanded to schools and communities in the state. Dr. Vander Mey also is involved in a farmer participatory development project in Ghana, West Africa.

Public Health and Parks, Recreation & Tourism

Jennifer L. Hinton (principle author) is a doctoral student in Recreation Therapy at Clemson University. Her interests include learning and facilitating teaching techniques that promote new ways of understanding for herself and her students.

Francis A McGuire (co-author) is a Professor in the Parks, Recreation, and Tourism Management Department at Clemson University. He teaches in therapeutic recreation and gerontology with research interests including intergenerational programming and therapeutic aspect of humor.

Judith S. Witthoeft (co-author) currently teaches the Health Promotion of the Aged class in the Public Health Department at Clemson University. Her research has been in the areas of nutrition, cardiac rehabilitation, and attitudes among older populations. Previously she was director of the Geriatric Studies at McDonough District Hospital, assistant to the president of Care Management Long term Care Services, and Nursing Service Administrator at Mercy Hospital.

Jessyna M. McDonald (co-author) has directed several projects on aging, health, and recreation. She has held postdoctoral fellowships from the National Institute on aging and the Gerontological Society of America. She has several publications and national presentations in applied gerontology.

Debra L. Mitchell (co-author) coordinated the service learning projects in this study while completing her Bachelor of Health Sciences degree. She is currently working toward a Masters of Professional Communication degree with an emphasis in health communication.

Marketing

Patricia A. Knowles is an Associate Professor in the Marketing Department at Clemson University. Dr. Knowles earned her B.A. in Psychology from Michigan State University and her M.A. and Ph.D. in Experimental/Physiological Psychology from Bowling Green State University. Finally, she completed a Post-Doc in Marketing at the University of Georgia. She has numerous published articles including those in the Journal of Nonprofit and Public Sector Marketing, the Journal of Marketing Management, the Journal of the Academy of Marketing Science, the Journal of Personal Selling and Sales Management and Pharmacology, Biochemistry & Behavior.

Organizational Communication

Steven J. Madden is an Assistant Professor in the Department of Speech & Communication Studies at Clemson University. Dr. Madden earned a B.A. in Mass Communications/Public Relations from the University of South Florida, an M.A. in Communication Studies/ Conflict Management from New Mexico State University, and a Ph.D. in Speech Communication/ Organizational Communication with a minor in Management from the University of Southern Mississippi. His expertise is in the area of organizational communication, conflict management, and mediation. He has taught 23 different courses dedicated to creating an applied environment where students actively utilize their academic knowledge in real-world applications. He currently has 7 journal publications, 2 workbooks, 2 chapters and 1 edited book.

Business Writing

Elizabeth C. Rice has taught at Clemson University for four years in the English department. While at Clemson, she has taught Business and Technical Writing, Writing and International Trade, American Literature, and Contemporary Literature. She incorporates service learning concepts and projects into all of her curricula. She was also the Director of Clemson University's America Reads program for the first two years of its existence.

Science

John R. Wagner, Professor of Geology, has taught a variety of geology and earth science courses at Clemson University since arriving in South Carolina in 1976. Prior to that time he taught at the secondary level in Pennsylvania for three years. He has been heavily involved in science outreach activities to schools and has coordinated a variety of professional development opportunities for both preservice and inservice teachers. He is a past-president of the National Association of Geoscience Teachers and a co-author of the award-winning SC MAPS middle school curriculum project.

Erik R. Caldwell, Visiting Instructor of Geology, recently received an M.S. degree in hydrogeology from Clemson University. In addition to teaching a variety of laboratory courses, he has become increasingly involved with the educational outreach efforts of the Department of Geological Sciences and has worked with Dr. Wagner on the SC MAPS curriculum as well as on several service learning projects.

Education

Carol G. Weatherford, Ed.D., is an Associate Professor at Clemson University in the Department of Educational Foundations and Special Education. She developed and taught a course for master;s level teachers called Integrating Service-Learning Across Curricula. Weathorford served on the Clemson University Service-Learning Committee and currently serves on the Clemson University Service-Learning Collaborative. She provided leadership in the development, implementation, and evaluation of Visions for Youth, a program that involves high-risk preadolescents in service-learning activities.

Emma M. Owens, Ed.D., is Associate Professor of Education in the Department of Curriculum and Instruction at Clemson University. Dr. Owens has taught mathematics on all educational levels, arithmetic through calculus, statistics, and probabililty. She has developed and taught courses for elementary school teachers of mathematics. While on a two-year leave of absence, she oversaw all assessment of student learning projects in the Elementary, Secondary, and Informal Education Division of the National Science Foundation, and was responsible for proposals, budgets, and continuations for Curriculum Development projects in K-12 mathematics. Service learning as a teaching methodology is one of her current research interests. She is also working on strategies and techniques for recruiting and retaining minorities, especially black males, into teaching.

Technical Writing

Barbara E. Weaver has taught writing and literature courses at Clemson University since January 1996. Prior to joining Clemson's English department facµlty, she worked as an information products developer and project leader for AT&T Corporation. She also worked as a freelance writer and photographer for several newspapers.

Acknowledgements

The total number of persons and organizations that made these projects and this book possible list in the hundreds. I apologize up-front for all of those who may not be represented here for one reason or another but please know that your contributions and efforts have had a positive effect on countless lives. Forgive me for not mentioning each name but I thank you deeply.

Editorial Assistance
Cassandra R. Bernard, Joseph Arndt, Jr., Beverly Holton.

Overall Service Learning Project Assistance
Clemson University Service Learning Collaborative and the National Dropout Prevention Center.

Individual and Organizational Service Learning Participants (partial listing)

Heather Caraskaden, National Wildlife Federation; Joe Dickerson, Pickens County Habitat for Humanity Property Chairman; Juliet Fletcher, South Carolina Wildlife Federation; Angela Viney, South Carolina Wildlife Federation; Craig Tufts, National Wildlife

Federation; Arlene Young, City of Clemson Community Development Specialist; Students: Tommy Bennett, Elliot Buff, Michael Church, Lee Cline, Joel Dellicarpini, Kelly Dralle, Natasha Larson, Bert Lynn, Jenny New, Sean Paone, Jamie Sittig, Jason Whinghter, Drew Alexander, Cathy Butler, Clay Carter, Michelle Edens, Alan Estes, Kristien Evans, Monica Mullis, Joshua Murdock, Ana Paz, Kevin Reed, Jessica Rockwell, Brent Shuler, Brian Smith, Matthew Stannis, Cheney Taylor, Chris Waters, Jason Whinghter, Shawn Whitman, Kathryn Wood, Brian Adams, Brent Bagwell, George Bell, John Blackmon, Andy Burton, Clay Carter, Chris Caruso, Troy Clymer, Kevin Conaway, Steven Culpepper, James Dargan, Kim Drawdy, Jennifer Dukes, Susan England, Aaron English, Alan Estes, Tim Henderson, Veronda Holcombe, Anna Hopkins, Mike Kelly, Janette Macdonald, Sian McDonald, Jennifer Merrell, Joshua Murdock, Leigh Murray, Zach Parker, Patrick Pruitt, Erik Rodgers, Caroline Schreier, Brian Schumpert, Abana Scott, Bill Scott, Christina Smith, Heidi Storey, Chris Waters, Adam White, Crystal White, Heather Wolfe, Josh Reed, Ryan Goff, Karl Muzii, Patricia Davis, Dr. Mary Davis, Dr. Maggie Emery, Dr. Shelley Fones, Dr. Lillian Hart, Dr. Rebecca Kaminski, Dr. Bea Naff, Ms. Cathy Sparks, Ms. Nancy Wilkinson, Brian Bauer, Angela Clark, Kraig Conley, Erin Deanhardt, Greg Jawski, James Leniham, Kyra Lutz, Kathrine McAllister, Marta McGough, Kim Murphy, James Romesburg, Brian Ruschli, Amanda Severance, Alexander Starkman, Nyoka Sullivan, Susanna Talchik, Tara Thigpin, Francis Thomas, Karin Thomas, Chris Todaro, Andrea White, Brandon Smith, Cristy Cato, Jeff Chan, Emily Daigre, Jason Gentry, Katherine Hughs, Kelly Jarrett, Jared March, Kerri McGuire, Patrick Nitsche, Kristen Nivica, McKenzie Obrien, Jody Phillips, John Sherer, Christopher Smith, Robert Strelick, Karlyn Thompson, Brucie Weavil, Emily Jones, Wendy Wieselberg, and Hayne McCall.